Celebrate Life

Viva La Vida

Namaya

Copyright © 2017 Namaya
All rights reserved

No Part of this publication may be reproduced, stored in a retrieval system, or transmitted in any form or by any means—electronic, mechanical, photocopy, recording, or any other—except for brief quotations in printed reviews, without the prior permission of the author.

Disclaimer: The Publisher and the Author make no representations or warranties with respect to the accuracy or completeness of the contents of this work and specifically disclaim all warranties, including without limitation warranties of fitness for a particular purpose. No warranty may be created or suitable for every situation. This work is sold with the understanding that the publisher is not engaged in rendering legal, accounting, or other professional services. If professional assistance is required, the services of a competent professional person should be sought. Neither the Publisher nor the Author(s) shall be liable for damages arising herefrom. The fact that an organization or website is referred to in this work as a citation and/or a potential source of further information does not mean that the Author or Publisher endorses the information the organization or website may provide or recommendations it may make. Further, readers should be aware that internet websites listed in this work may have changed or disappeared between when this work was written and when it is read.

Published by Vermont Art Poetry Press
773 Guilford Street
Brattleboro, VT 05301

ISBN-13: 978-0-9990844-6-5

Dedicated to my friend and mentor

Ross Trentacosti

Artist, teacher, & bonvivant.

Contents

Introduction

Yes, to life! Yes -- to the extraordinary possibilities life offers! What inspires you? What is your manifesto in life? What satisfies you profoundly -- to the bone? "Celebrate Life" is a collection of stories and anecdotes about my journey in life.

They're stories of the kindness of people, coping with family and disappointment, and ultimately celebrating and living this amazing life. When people ask me how I am - I say in all sincerity, "If life gets any better, I'm going to have to give it a refund."

I come from a working class family. My father was a mechanic and he worked hard for his living that was reflected in his scarred and calloused hands. He was a dutiful man, whose life focused on work and family.When I was a fifteen I met a man, to whom this book is dedicated, Ross Trentacosti, an artist, who was the same age as my dad. Ross worked, but he had fun, played and delighted in the friendship of others. I valued my father's work ethic, but I emulated Ross and his joie de vivre.

I worked full-time since I was seventeen and part-time since I was fourteen. I joined the Navy at seventeen and then when I got out I worked at nights and went to college during the day. With some help from the GI Bill, I was able to afford college. I've worked as a teacher, LPN, RN, homeopath, performance poet, Family Nurse Practitioner, organizational consultant, 3rd World Development specialist, handyman, artist, Peace Corps volunteer, and a host of trades and professions. Since I was twenty, I've written poetry and stories, and found the time each day to create. I make my art because it is as essential to me as breathing, even if it meant waking up hours earlier before my "day job." I had always struggled to find that balance between paying the bills and making my art. I've now created a life where my needs are modest and I can spend more time doing what I love to do best– creating, doing community service projects, and enjoy life with my wife Zoe and the people we love. By living simply and focusing on what I really enjoy, I'm much happier. I thought work had to be difficult and make me feel miserable, but I discovered as I got older that I had a choice and work could be fun.

CHAPTER 1

The Real Revolution

in the 21st century the ultimate act
of revolution is for a person
to wake up in the morning
and devote the day to writing
a poem or making art.

no cellphones, emails, etc.,

the world swirls around, jack hammers
roar, children in schools,
planes fly overhead, business people
on the run, babies in strollers, maids
washing clothes, and I am here...

making an impression on a sheet of
paper; one stroke,
one syllable,
one word at a time

For too many years, I jumped out of bed at the sound of the alarm clock and launched myself into the world. I slowly realized this was not the way I wanted to live my life. What works best for me is waking up slowly, having my breakfast without a radio, television, or cell phone sounding, and quietly starting the day. Even now, halfway through life, I'm still learning to find a gentler and less frenetic way of living. And, by doing less, I'm accomplishing more. The lines from William Blake's poem, "Auguries of Innocence," capture this sense of wonder and presence in the moment:

> *To see a World in a Grain of Sand*
> *And a Heaven in a Wild Flower*

Hold Infinity in the palm of your hand
And Eternity in an hour[1]

What is your intention in life? What is your fun? Why are you truly here? Beyond the expectations of family or friends, what is your truest passion in life?

This is the challenge and the choice for me. How do I create a life where I can pursue my true passion and joy? How do we dare to dream the dream of our lives and live it? *Celebrate Life: Viva La Vida* is the invitation to fully embrace your life and vision. How do we live a life with a joyful spirit?

Joy is not a giddy, ecstatic state of being, but rather it's about being fully present and awake to life. When I am attentive to the miracles of beauty that surround me -- from the dance of the wind across Blue Heron Pond at our home to the exquisite violet crocuses peering through the late spring snow -- the more open I am to the true possibility of life.

Joy is a life of passion, intention, and celebration. I celebrate this miracle of life in all the ways that it comes – sad or joyful, with all its doubts, ambiguities, and disappointments. All of this is the mix in *Celebrate Life*.

Dare to be a *rEvolutionary*. Dare to be extraordinary! Discover the enchantment in your daily life.

Celebrate life! Viva la Vida! Celebrate ***your*** life.

Yes!

Namaya
2017

---

1 *Auguries of Innocence* by William Blake

Ask For What You Want

What is your true passion and joy in life? Is it a life of travel and discovery? Are you happiest working in the community and serving the needy? Do you want to get up on stage to sing and dance? Is your joy your family and home, and raising your kids? There are many wonderful choices you can make, but what is the one (or more) that makes you the happiest and gives you the deepest contentment?

When I was a homeopathic physician, I did an exercise with patients to help them visualize the life they wanted. Not the life they *should or ought to pursue*, but a life that was profoundly satisfying to them.

This is a visualization that you can do yourself. Imagine a *house of many rooms.* In this house, each room represents a year of your life. If you are twenty years old, the house has twenty-one rooms, and if you are fifty years old, the house has fifty-one rooms, etc. The house might be anywhere in the world; perhaps it is in the Caribbean or in the mountains. But this is your house. Each room represents one year of your life. Some rooms are closed and some are filled with a lot of debris. We spend too much time in the rooms of the past… *old loves, missed chances, not good enough, not smart enough, not happy enough*… If you had a happy childhood, the rooms are filled with wonderful memories.

There is one extra room called NOW. This is the room of the present and the future that you truly want. You can have anyone or no one in this room. This room is the best and most idealized place for you. This room holds your favorite music and books, and maybe even a time machine to transport you to your fondest hopes. When you have the time and energy, you can empty out the old rooms, but the key is living in this one room of Now. What will you create?

An Aspiring Con Artist

At the age of three, my niece
was a quiet, thoughtful, and
kind child. Little did I suspect
her underlying tendencies.
We were on the boardwalk at
Venice Beach. I bought us each an
ice cream cone.
She finished hers quickly and
then asked, "Can I have a taste of yours?"
"Of course you can, dear."
She was soon devouring
my ice cream. Spying me waiting,
she paused and looked up at me
with her innocent brown eyes.
Then, after a tiny fake cough, she said,
"I can't give it back to you, I have a cold."

Be The Rose

I never expected miracles as a
homeopathic physician, but
I was open to the possibility.

A woman, came to see me,
An alcoholic, abused, and her
spirit seemed broken.

On her breast, rising up to her
collar bone, was a rose tattoo.

After two hours of listening
I gave her a homeopathic dose of *stramonium* –
a remedy, as I saw it, for "one who is lost in the
wilderness without their tribe."

I didn't expect to see her again.

About a year later, an attractive woman
came to my office and she said,
"You don't recognize me? I saw you about a
year ago and you gave me some small pills.
I didn't think much of it, but afterwards
I had a dream about how my life could be different.
and I didn't have to be a victim.
I didn't have to be trapped in the lies."

"Yes, I remember you, but you've blossomed."

"It's strange you said that, Doctor. Before I met you
I felt like the sludge in the sewer. Now I feel like

the rose growing from that sludge."

After she left, I looked up *stramonium* in my homeopathic reference book,
"Grows in refuse and dung heaps."

Be the rose.

Best Parents & Best Children

We were too old to have children
when we married, so we
focused our parental love on
our nieces and nephews.
and informally adopted other children along the way.

However, our best parenting has been to ourselves.
We became *parents to ourselves,*
the parents we wish we could have had.

Those wonderful parents are superb!
They're very loving and kind, with lots of hugs.
They're rarely grumpy and offer plenty of
time for us kids to play and dream.

They give us exotic journeys to fill our wanderlust,
buy us lots of books, take us to museums, and give us enough
allowance for our special toys – guitars, art stuff, and more.

As *children*, in turn, we're the best kids parents could want!
We're very loving and kind and give lots of hugs.
We're mostly obedient when the occasion
suits us and generally happy.
We require only love,
kindness,
and time to
dream.

We are the parents to ourselves.
We are the children to those wonderful parents.

Life Is Just The Way It Is

1

Take it as it comes
See what you become
Be the best if you dare
But only if you care

If you're in for revolution
Do your <u>own</u> evolution
Fly down from the trees
Crawl among the fleas

Get a fateful itch
To make the switch
And live your life
Without such strife

2

Cry for the pain
Dance in the rain!
Choose what you do
It's all up to you

Whine or complain
Or sip champagne
Only you can change
The links of your chain

Cry, laugh, or dance
Life is short, take a chance
Kiss a beautiful stranger
Life, is worth the danger

3

Try a new attitude
Or live with gratitude
An attitude of gratitude
May lend needed altitude

Life is cruel or kind
Don't pay it no mind
A change of season
Will change that reason

Hide away underground
Or claim the highest ground
Embrace the loneliest fear
Or live outrageous & clear

4

Take it as it comes
See what you become
Be the best if you dare
But only if you care

Reach for your life
Dance on the edge of a knife
Celebrate it complete
Life bitter & sweet

Win, draw, or lose
It's what you choose.
Live large, blow a fuse
If you wish just refuse

Life is just the way it is
It's all up to you.

Sophia Loren At The Ice Cream Store

When I was a young
teenage boy a
beautiful buxom
woman in a dress
two sizes too small
and generous
cleavage would
bend over the ice
cream counter to scoop
out a serving.

One scoop, two,
and one more
at the front
where she would
have to lean
all the way
over towards my
famished eyes
as I drank in
those luscious
velvety curves
of desire ready
to melt on my
tongue.
"Would there be anything else, love?" she'd ask as she handed me a towering ice-cream cone.

"Yes, would you
be able to put on

some sprinkles?"

For the finale,
the coup de grace,
the consummation
of the feast

she'd lean over
the counter to
reach the sprinkles
and the generous
scoops threatened
to topple over as
she adorned my
ice cream cone.

P.S.
I'm allergic to ice cream; nevertheless,
faithfully, every week during the summer
I bought an ice cream cone and gave it to a friend.

What Is Your Mission In Life?

Some people have a hard time
figuring out their
raison d'être – their mission.

Me?
Irascible rabble rouser?
Creative revolutionary?

Artist 4 Peace?
Homeopath – healer,
        Jazz Poet—dancing
                on the high wire of improvisation?

Community organizer?
        Tennis junkie?
                Life, learning, travel, & culture lover?

I am all that and then some.

And for you,

What is your mission statement in life?

What Is Your Allegory Of The Cave?

Which do we live – the true life or the life of shadow? Do we hold to our illusion or do we live fearlessly? This is the question that has been asked since the time of Socrates and before. What is the true life?

In *Allegory of the Cave* by Plato, people are chained to the wall of a cave. There is a fire in the cave and they see their lives as the shadows on the walls. One prisoner escapes and, on leaving, is blinded by the sun. Gradually, he regains his sight, but, as his eyes adjust to the light, he realizes that he has been seeing the world of shadow and illusion.

The *Allegory of the Cave* invites us to consider which life we choose: the life and career preferred by our parents, the career that generates the most money, or the house with the most prestige -- or do we choose a life that we truly want?

Imagine a world where people followed their true passion and pursued those things that deeply motivate them.

Thoreau, in *On Civil Disobedience*, said, "Most men lead lives of quiet desperation and go to the grave with their song still in them."

And for you, how do you discover your true passion and live your fondest aspirations? How do you truly live the beautiful dream of your life?

CHAPTER 2

CARPE DIEM: SEIZE THE DAY

The Latin adage *Carpe Diem* means "Seize the day!" Take each day and make it as extraordinary as you can. Even in your most difficult moments, when life and work seem to overwhelm you, find the present extraordinary moment, and savor it. When life is calm and perhaps too quiet, savor the tranquility. Carpe Diem – Seize the day!

There is a Zen story about a man running from a bear. The bear is getting closer, the man arrives at the edge of a cliff with a thousand-foot drop. At the bottom is a tiny river. He leaps and grabs a vine halfway down. There is a moment of sheer joy as he realizes he escaped death! Then he sees a lion at the bottom of the ravine. He holds on to the vine, savoring the sun and the moment of safety, when he notices a mouse nibbling at the vine he's holding on-to. There is a strawberry growing nearby, he grabs it and bites into it. It's the most delicious berry he has ever eaten.

Seize your day! Celebrate the paradox, the joy, and all of life.

I was sitting on the marble church steps on the grand canal of Venice at sunset. I watched the incredible lustrous orange sun setting, the orchestra inside the church playing a Vivaldi concerto. I was spell-bound by the glorious sunset and the music. Even twenty years later, that perfect moment is still vivid in my mind.

Now, in the early autumn of Vermont, I turn off my cell phone, the computers, and all the extraneous noise inside my head. I watch the dance of autumn leaves and enjoy the smell of wood stoves burning as I savor the cool breeze dancing across Blue Heron Pond. I breathe.

Living in the moment doesn't take wealth or education, only the willingness to set aside the cell phone, turn off the television and chatter around you, and simply be awed by the world. Each one of us has the capacity and ability to experience the miracle of life and the beauty of the world.

Carpe diem! Seize the day!

I Don't Punch The Clock

I don't work 9 to 5,

but as an artist and writer
my clock runs 24/7 365 days
of the year.

It could be the middle of
the night or in the middle
of loving… when the inspiration
strikes…with pen, paint, or
a poem.

365 days of the year
I am attentive to the possibility
of creating.

I don't punch the clock,
but when I wake up
my mind and spirit
are alive and I'm ready to create.

I'm making the time
to do what I want and need
to do and that is

to create.

Best Boyhood Summer

There is a place for swimming,
running, hiking, and doing other
boyhood things,

but my favorite summer nook
was in the old library at my
hometown.

The librarian who knew me smiled,
and handed me a book as I walked in,
"You'll like this one."

In the far back recesses was an
old leather couch worn to
a buttery soft comfort by
decades of readers.

I put my shoes on the floor,
pool towel beside me,
stretched out and dived
into the cascade of fiction and history.

The library smelled of
well-read books as I nestled
into the couch for that long
hot summer afternoon, while
I was cool and swimming in
my imagination.

When I came home my mother
asked, "How was the pool today?"

"I couldn't have
imagined a better day."

First Taste

The first cup

not the hurried one
on the train or to work
not the second or third
nor the espresso after lunch squeezed
in to make it through
to the end of the day.

The first cup

avored slow
reverentially mindful
as a monk, each sip
a slow revelation to
wakening

Bagel Memory

This morning I sat down to eat
a poppy seed bagel with butter.

I remembered when
I was broke and hungry,

and the luxury of a toasted bagel with butter
and a cup of coffee made me feel rich.

This morning, I savored each bite slowly.
Now, as then, I feel
like the richest man in all the world.

Flying Captain: Look Before You Leap?

While working in the Intensive Care Unit at a NYC hospital, I met the captain of a sixty-foot sail boat who had just completed a solo trip from the south of France to New York City.

The day before, he was sleeping in his fifth floor apartment in New York City, when, in the middle of the night, the air conditioner began to rattle. He got up, half-asleep, and adjusted the air conditioner. With one hand, he lifted the window up, causing the AC to tumble downwards. He reached out and grabbed it. The AC fell out of the window with him trailing behind, landing five stories below. He was found on the sidewalk lying on top of the shattered machine. When he woke up in the intensive care unit, with a fractured hip and two fractured shoulders, he looked up at the faces of his wife and surgeon and asked, "How is the air conditioner?"

The wife, smiling and then crying said, "You fared better than it did."

Miracle

if

we beheld
each drop
of water
as a tear from
the eye of
god

if
we savored
each breath
of wind

if
this is the earth
where the
Buddha sits

if
this second
was your very
last and you
had the eternity
of time to savor

if

Faced With The Financial Consequence Of Writ I-N-G

Monday morning,
and I'm sitting in bed
with a cup of coffee,
my pen and paper,
on a cold rainy
day and writing poems.

Not necessarily big
or fancy poems, your
everyday kind of poems
about being and living.

I'm fully aware
that I could be
off to the
alleged *real work* of
the world:

Building a house,
making bombs,
baking a cake,
making money,
selling real estate, etc.,

instead of spending
the morning
writ I N G a poem.

Far happier
work I NG
and BE I N G

a poet at his trade.

October Reminder

October blows in with its
windy bluster, tempting
hints of sun, invitations of
gold and red, and inundations
of rain. All reminders --
gather wood, clean the
furnace and stove, turn off the
outside faucets, mend the
roof, seal and patch the cracks,
store extra water and food,
new candles, stock up on
kerosene and lamp oil, the
hundred score things that
still need to be done, but
the task most important--

is to hold every ounce of
memory of the full summer
sun as it warms my soul

Precious Time

An odd spring,

one day
t-shirt and
shorts
weather,
then the
next,
cold.

Today
wrapped
in winter
jackets
Zoe and I
walked
in the woods
by the pond.

We found a
sunlit spot
by the stream
and laid down.

My head
resting on her
tummy
as we watched
clouds
amble by

and fell asleep
as the nascent
spring grew
beneath us.

Snowflake Bourbon

Cold night

Step outside
with a glass of
bourbon
on the porch

Snowflakes
fall and drift

a few land in
the glass--
better than ice

Air warms
the bourbon

Slowly it
evaporates
to heaven

Angels
smile

Before I Go

Before I die

I will savor
every instant
of joy and life,

and wring out every
ounce of creative juice
from this being.

My bones and gristle,
to make a savory
bone soup of dreams.

The blood becomes
paint for my canvas.

Every dream and vision,
a strand to this weaving.

The Reluctant Virgins Of Venice

She was a twenty-one-year-old blond
German woman I met at the Venice train station.
She said to me,
"Would you like to share a room? But no hanky-panky."
"No, hanky-panky?"
"Yes, we share only the room. You have one bed and
I have the other one. Understood?"
The Teutonic sternness got me all excited, plus she
was kind of cute and I was sure she would
succumb to my charms.

It was the weekend of her birthday and Venice was
warm and sunny in early May. That night
we made our way to the hotel in Campo San Margherita.

Our room was barely big enough for the
queen-sized bed. With the best of intentions,
I leaped in, and she jumped in on the other side.
However, the bed was older than the both of us and it
sagged under the weight of generations of lovers.
As we sank into the middle of the bed,
she said, "No, hanky-panky!"
We slept that night, arms around each other like lovers, but
our glorious weekend in Venice was chaste.
Or, at least, that's what she said.

A happy birthday weekend, indeed.

To The Last Atom

A man I had been having
a disagreement with about
a local political issue was
riding a bike down the road.

I was in my car and in the
back of my mind I thought,
I'd nudge him with my car.

The thought was playful,
the anger apparent,
but I had the insight that I wanted
to live long enough so that the
last ounce of violence, the last
atom of anger was dissipated
and gone before I died.

At that moment, he saw my
car, smiled and waved to me
as I drove by.

CHAPTER 3

CAVEAT EMPTOR- BUYER BEWARE

Buyer beware. Whether it is a handkerchief, a car, a relationship, or any kind of transaction, these words resonate: *Buyer beware.* What is your responsibility as a consumer? Have you done your due diligence or, like I tend to do, have you fallen head over heels in love with a car and bought it on the spot? Ooops!

Which purchase did you regret? That dream cottage on the lake that you justified by saying, "Don't worry, it's my dream cottage." And then you found out it's sitting in a flood zone… Oops!

Love is another one of those inexplicable categories. You think that the new love of your life will change your world. And then you find that your soul mate has a rap sheet of bad romances, hard luck, and more sad stories than you possibly could have imagined. Oops!

It's remarkable, but the clichés are true. If something looks too good to be true, it probably is. Think of Bernie Madoff, or any one of the hucksters and con artists who have sauntered through your life.

When Ernest Hemmingway was asked what the key was to being a good writer, he said, "A great crap detector." The same applies to life! The secret to living a successful life is having a great crap detector.

The simple truth that has stood the test of time is simply, *Caveat Emptor!* Yes, *Buyer Beware…* Be very wary, indeed!

Kitchen Cabinets

It started quite simply as simple things do in life. I needed a place to put my dishes, silverware, and pots. The pine shelves with the tacky plaid contact paper now appeared a bit outdated. I went to the kitchen store and there were many ways to store pots, pans, forks, knives, and the gazillion gadgets that people use for kitchens.

I was lost and confused by the plethora of choices at the store. I asked the young salesman, “Excuse me, my friend. I would like a simple nice looking cabinet for a few plates, pots, and silverware.”

“Preposterous!” declared the salesman, who looked suspiciously at my patched jeans. “A man of your education and style needs something befitting your status in life.”

His point was difficult to argue with. He showed me the first choice, a mahogany cabinet from an organic farm in an eco-preserve forest, harvested by unionized disabled workers. The drawers had titanium ball bearings handcrafted in Switzerland by Eritrean political refugees, and they provided a flawless glide for the drawers. Who could argue with such impeccable precision and political correctness?

“The best choice is a teak cabinet designed by a Swede living in a biosphere in the rain forest of Costa Rica,” insisted the salesman.

“You’re a great salesman,” I said.

The salesman was quick to correct me, “I’m not a salesman, but a culinary interior designer.”

“Oh, really?”

My desire for a few simple cabinets where I could store my dishes was quickly exposed as an anachronistic attachment to a Luddite puerility that could be attributed only to some unfulfilled attachment to my working class roots. This was carefully pointed out by the psychosocial assessment that I was compelled to fill out when I came into the store.

"Sir," said the culinary interior designer with a wry, smug, little twitter, "This is a far too complicated choice for you to discern—the colors, the textures, the granite countertops milled from mountaintops in Vermont, the artistic quality of the layers of fine Chinese lacquer on the silverware drawer, and the hundred-and-one other critical choices are best left to my expertise. Wouldn't you agree?"

I was dumbfounded! The teak, the mahoganies, the titanium hardware, the exotic woods culled from organic sustainable forests, and the other exquisite options that I could barely comprehend, quickly translated into a delighted "Voila!" from the culinary interior designer.

"Sir, we have prices that will more than suit your modest budget. We'll have the craftsman flown in to install your kitchen cabinets, and, for the modest one-hundred-forty-thousand-dollar investment, we'll include a set of antique Irish linens," he said with a glint in his eye and a smile on his face that was somewhere between the bemused grin of an assassin and the wide-eyed devotion of a religious acolyte.

I felt a cold sweat running down my neck that seeped onto the immaculate embossed estimate as I backed slowly out of the door. "Let me think about this. I'm sure… this is a terrific deal."

"Sir, this offer won't last long! He who hesitates is lost!" called out the culinary interior designer from the bowels of the store.

Trembling and making my way through the back alley to my car, my head was swimming with images of beautiful mahogany and teak cabinets, when I tripped over some packing crates lying in the alley. One was stamped, "Near genuine mahogany kitchen cabinets from China. Some assembly required."

An epiphany enveloped me as I beheld those soft pine packing crates, and I tied them to the roof rack of my car. As I drove off, the culinary interior designer called out, "Sir, we'll include a set of knives made by a family of samurai craftsmen!"

After sanding, refinishing with linseed oil, and mounting the pine crates to the kitchen wall, I carefully placed my heirloom china from the Salvation Army on top, next to the forks and spoons. A row of polished stout nails nicely held my pots in place.

My Ravenous Marilyn In The French Quarter

I was a young sailor who got off from
work at 5p.m on Friday,
and me and my buddies drove from
Jacksonville to the Big Easy in
about seven hours.

Bourbon Street was alive with all kinds
of drinking and bad boy behavior!
I'm sure I bumped and bruised
a few things, but I didn't feel
any pain – however, I remember all
the beautiful women I met at
this one night club..

In my rum soaked mind, I knew the women had a
voracious desire for me, and I was only too happy
to accommodate.
I winked to my friend and tossed him
the car keys,
"I'll see you back at the room."

She had a Marilyn Monroe
voluptuousness that inspired
my dreams of rapture.

When we turned the corner
she said in a sensuous whisper,
"I can't wait any longer,
let's do it here in the Alley."

Stupefied and inebriated, I said,
        "Splendid idea!"

She threw me up against the wall,
voluptuous breasts rubbing against me
and slurpy deep tongue kisses,
        when in the midst of an
impending orgiastic reverie I felt the firm
        throbbing pole of her manhood
about to pierce my innocence.

"Damn," I thought with rare lucidity.
"I got to stop drinking so much."

I remember Marilyn under the street
        lights with such tender innocence.

The Toilet Seat

Everything I needed to understand about life, economics, and recycling I learned from my toilet seat.

A toilet seat is not a very elegant topic for an essay, but, if we can be candid, it's a subject that's dear to many of our hearts and points beyond. My toilet seat was getting a bit rickety. It's a firm oak seat, nicely polished, but the screws were falling out, and I thought maybe I could get one of those luxurious soft plastic seats - and maybe even one that was heated! It gets cold on those Vermont winter nights. Though it doesn't compare to the toilet my friend in NYC has that lowers the seat, washes your bottom with a warm soapy spray, and then blows you dry. Your hands never have to touch your body. Nevertheless, my concerns are far more pedestrian when it comes to this creaky oak toilet seat.

I went down to the hardware store and there was a rack of plastic, padded, and oak seats, and even a heated one. I evaluated them in terms of comfort, durability, and where they were manufactured. I'm particular about where I park some of my most valuable terrain. Most were made in China, but I'm trying to avoid buying products from China whenever possible. I found my choices reduced to mahogany models from Brazil. Given my reticence to import toilet seats from exotic locales merely to meet the all-important needs of my posterior, I was in a quandary. The matter of what I sit on in the morning for my constitutional may be of interest only to me; nevertheless, wars have been waged over far less. I realized this wasn't a decision I could take lightly and that this problem required careful deliberation.

I returned to the seat of my throne and connected with my primal soul. Though the seat creaked and groaned a bit, I realized that my antiquated toilet seat suited me just fine. Sometimes it's important to put our ass on the line for ecology.

Dennis And Bob

My friend Dennis and I were drinking at a bar and having a jolly good time when suddenly a woman walked in. She was quite attractive. She looked at Dennis andsaid, “Bob, how ya’ doing?”

Despite his confusion, he started to have a lovely chat with this woman. As things happen in life, Dennis and Melissa were getting along splendidly. As they left the bar Dennis said to me, “I guess I’ll see you tomorrow.”

I had lunch the next day with Dennis, who was still nursing a hangover. “So, Dennis, tell me, how did your date go last night?” He laughed so hard he fell to the floor.. “You wouldn’t believe it!”

“Try me.”

“We went back to her apartment and had a great time last night.”

“And, so what was the problem?”

“In the morning, she asked, “Bob, you want coffee?”

“Sure thing, baby.”

“After a few minutes she came back with two coffees. According to Dennis she looked bewildered, dazed, and terrified all in one moment. She dropped the two coffees on the floor and said, “You’re not Bob! Who are you?”

Crap Detector

When Ernest Hemmingway
was asked what was the best tool
for a writer. He said,
"A great crap detector."

What kind of crap detector do you have?

Is it a tiny shy one that
that goes *chirp chirp*
when a new love comes by and
whispers, *I love you*?

Does your crap detector
have a Geiger counter
kind of *bip-bip-bip*
that reacts loudly
when a force of bullshit
comes into range?

Or does it go off when
you hear about the best
investment deal of your life—
the 35% return on
investment that can
only be completed
---now!

Always, keep your
crap detector close at hand.

CHAPTER 4

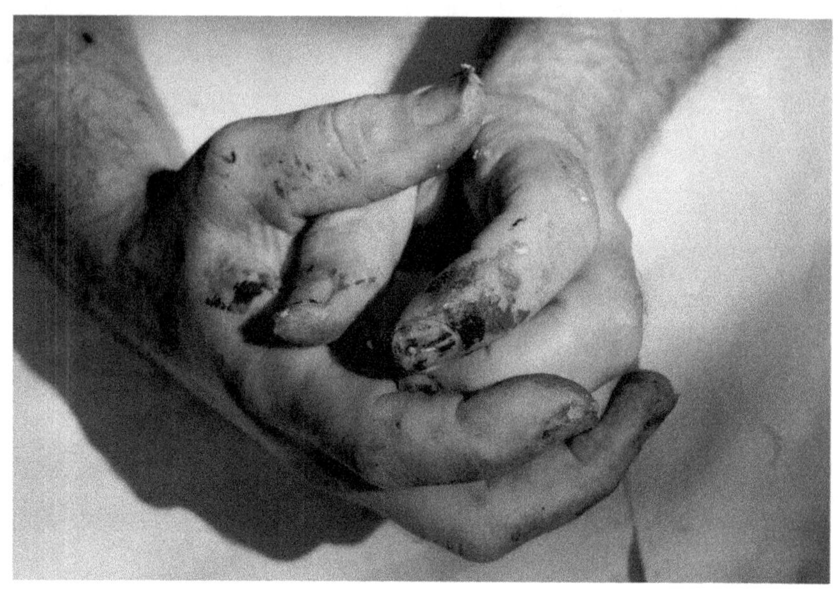

DIG YOUR CREATIVE SOUL!

Riding The Creative Dragon

The creative journey, whether as a painter, a poet, a dancer, or any one of the myriad artistic expressions, is about connecting to our profound capacity to imagine and create.

The creative journey has little to do with an MFA in art or poetry, or how much money you make or don't make..

In Malta last winter, I was at one of the oldest Neolithic sites in the world and there was a tiny clay-fired figurine of a pregnant woman. This icon represented an idea of beauty and simplicity that is so compelling.

When I was in eighth grade, a teacher told us to write a poem about clouds. I had never written a poem and I don't remember what I wrote. However, I remember the teacher scolding me for the poem and telling me how bad it was. It's ironic, I've spent most of my adult life writing and performing poetry.

In short, NEVER LISTEN TO THE CRITICS. Sure, it is vital to continue to develop your craft and skill, but don't let teachers or others put you and your art down. Write, draw, create, and dance your truth. Often, my art is about my thinking or exploration on a subject, and then, somewhere at the end, I realize it may be good enough to publish or present.

Though I love the accolades and applause, one of the the best applauses I had ever received was, "I was at your performance and heard the poem, *Life Is*. I was deeply depressed but I wrote down that poem, put it on my mirror, and that lifted my spirits." When my poetry or art can inspire someone, that is applause enough for me.

One my greatest *payment* from my friend, the great poet Hayden Carruth. Hayden was very elderly and I performed one of his poems, though he was in ill health, he creakily stood up to give me a standing ovation. I could not have been more honored.

I cherish poetry that inspires and speaks to the deepest level of our humanity: art that makes us wonder, dance that makes us get up and swing, photography that opens our eyes, and jazz that causes us to soar. Not the paintings that cost a gazillion dollars, but the art that exists in the every day.

Ride your creative dragon.

Driving With Hayden Carruth

"I don't talk much." Hayden said.

After an hour of quiet
driving towards Middlebury
for the next reading, a snippet
of conversation leads to
jazz sessions in Chicago and
New York … Teagarden,
Pee Wee Russell, Chick
Webb, Condon, Goodman,
and the memory of hundreds of jazz
players who have fused their
silken driving rhythms into
the pores of Hayden's poems.

His oxygen tank clicks
mechanically every 15 seconds,
the soulless backbeat
maintains life, it becomes
a thread in our conversation.
Words are measured carefully--
they are the lifeblood.

"Hayden, what makes a good poem?"

"Genuineness. Genuine to the
feeling and intent, without
all the editorializing."

Then we fall into
silence, driving through
the snow and rain, the
oxygen pulses.

Imperative

I will never
draw a line
like Picasso;

never steal the
sun like Van Gogh;

nor capture the
eloquence of love
in stone like Rodin.

The impossibly exquisite
geometry of Dali
will elude me,
but I will never fear
the fragile beauty
of creation.

My colors are drawn
from the well
of longing and desire.

My palette of dreams
forged from the fire
of my art and life.

I will create
from my
soul's truest
longing.

Avocation For David Budbill

Some need to be the head of the
band, drumming and marching.

Some folks lead the revolt
humming and storming.

Others are content in the garden
weeding and raking the beds.

Some don't even stir from their
beds, drinking tea and dreaming.

Me, the poet cat, I spend my day
singing with the universe,

gaze into space, writing poems,
slowly,

one poem,

one word,

at a time

Mfa Assimilating The Economics Of Life

"My MFA is in
poetry…
the **leading**
MFA program."
he said firmly while giving
me the change
for a taxi ride.

Then
the taxi slipped away
into a stream of similes
and metaphors.

Mining For The Poem

day after day, painfully
ordinary --a laborer
tied to the task at hand;
year in and out, scraping
away, digging deeper,
sifting through the tailings:

brutish work, hunched shoulders
and working with the coarse tools of
intellect and insight.

then, if lucky,
a shard of a gem in the midst of
a ton of debris; dull, easy to
miss, nearly impossible
to find and hold. Up from the
mines, smoothed, refined, and
with exquisite attention, held to
the light.

My First Play And Learning The Ropes As A Playwright

I was in the fourth grade and we were asked to write a play. I had never seen a play, but when the teacher explained it, I said, "I can write a play!"

It was in 1964, about six months after JFK was assassinated, and I knew of only one profound event in my lifetime. I wrote a one-page story and gave it to the teacher. I explained with great pride and enthusiasm how the car scene would play out, with the President shot, and the car racing off the stage. My teacher's eyes widened, and I thought I had made an effective pitch. She said quietly, "We were thinking more of a children's play."

One of the first and most important lessons for a playwright and artist, is to learn to deal with rejection -- and producers -- with a myopic perspective.

My Grateful Fans

The first few hours of the day
I write poems, play guitar,
draw or paint…however, the muse speaks.

My fans patiently await
as I sit on the back
porch by Blue Heron Pond.

The maple trees in their
luxuriant summer garments
are patiently attentive.

The purple and pink lilacs
appreciatively wave.

Bright yellow chrysanthemums
are joyfully
brilliant in their excitation.

The sky opens wide
with blue surprise
at each fresh creation

My poems,
stories,
art,
and
music

are eagerly received

by all.

My fans by the
hundred score

are attentive and appreciative of
my every creation.

Poets And Social Graces

Dylan Thomas, a boor and a drunk, wrote
poems that would make the angels jealous.

Ginsberg, Beat poet, lusty Buddhist monk,
compelled us to put our shoulder to the wheel.

Ezra, despite flawless modern cantos,
a fascist dancing in the thick of bigotry.

Cavalier poets-- young men addicted to
swordplay, drink, lust and short lives.

But in the midst of it all-- drugs, alcohol,
laudanum, depravity… there is -- genius.

A desire like Prometheus to bring fire
and illuminate the famished sight.

Seers, mystics, drunks, holy fools,
blessed saviors and tattered saints.

Prometheus

Poets
fly
off
buildings
and
drown
to
awaken

again

&

again.

The Aboriginal Painting Imperative

My cosmic egg shattered
when I saw the Aboriginal painting
in the Victoria Museum.

A canvas 12 feet long
of dots, snakes, spirals.

I didn't understand it.

Yet, I felt the painting pulse,
a message coming through,
animated and alive.

The painting said,
"Namaya, paint!"

I have not stopped
painting since.

The Richness Of Colored Pencils

I was excited as I looked
at the box of
12 expensive color Prisma
pencils in the window.

The salesgirl unlocked the case
and the world of
luxurious color pencils
were all there at
my finger's touch...

meadows of colors,
wild flowers blooming
in secret reveries and
fine drawings
of sleepy faces.

I couldn't afford such
luxuries as these pencils
when I was
younger.
I bought this set of 12 Prisma
colored pencils

and I felt like the
the most fortunate person.

The World Held Its Breath

I hadn't been painting.

My pastels had grown
ruddy and dull,
brittle.

My tubes of acrylic
with their
fire stolen from the sun,

greens of promise
and vermillion memories
were dreaming
like the fish in their
winter pond.

How does the memory
of sun keep alive
our dreams while we
are held in the prison
of our silence?

Whom Do I Write For?

… I write for the thousands
maybe millions of people
who imagined a poem, spoke
a phrase, rhymed a set of words,
chanted a bit of doggerel,
rapped or who lived their
life as a poem or story
that was never written.

Whom do I write for?

I write to save
my soul.

To Hell With Sentiment

angelic poems
with soft cadences
and exquisite
polished meter

that lilts and flows
with a caress and
subtle ease?

Hell, no!

I want to bite
a poem

and spit it back
to the universe.

CHAPTER 5

EMBRACING FAILURE AND FORGIVENESS

Our lives are filled with success and beautiful memories. Nevertheless, in every life there are extraordinary failures, near misses, and just plain old missed goals. We can be devastated and immobilized by these failures or pick ourselves up and take the next step.

Winston Churchill said, "Success is not final, failure is not fatal; it is the courage to continue that counts."

That is the key and the difference in the long term with success or failure. It is recognizing that, as Alexander Pope famously said, "To err is human; to forgive divine." It is easier sometimes for me to forgive another person, and more difficult to forgive myself. Yet, Churchill reminds us,

"Success consists of going from failure to failure without loss of enthusiasm."

Yes, embrace your failures as learnings, and celebrate the successes.

Regrets

There are regrets in my life—
missed meetings and chances,
fortunes that could have been
gained, money squandered, but
the regret that haunts me the most
is I did not spend enough time-
gazing idly at the moon.

Stupid Box

I saw a lovely scarf in a store-window
and I said to my friend,
"I have to buy this for my wife."

"Is it her birthday
or a special occasion?"

"No, it's for my stupid box."

"Stupid box?"

"Yes, I keep a box in my office
of various gifts for her in case I do
something egregiously stupid."

He smiled, "It must be a big box."

"Not exactly. I try to keep it as small
as possible."

Amish Girls -
Mercy And Forgiveness

October 2, 2006
Nickel Mines, Pennsylvania

I wept on hearing
the news of the five Amish
girls killed by a gunman.
and the other children wounded.

My soul wept for the
shameful insanity.

My soul burns for the
shame of being human.
After the last gun shot,
the children buried and
others cared for, the words
and actions of the Amish
were of forgiveness.

A depth of compassion
and forgiveness I find
difficult to fathom.

The faith of the Amish
community so powerful
that even this shooting
could not dissuade them
from their path of love
and forgiveness.

Now, many years since
this insanity, so many
more school killings and
war, and I am left humbled
by the courage of love.
In the face of death the older children tried to protect
the younger children.
"Shoot me, but not my sister."
said one girl.

Afterwards, the Amish community embraced
the killer's family with
forgiveness and love.

I remember these children
today –
and the courage of love.

Naomi Rose Ebersol
Marian Stoltzfus Fisher
Anna Mae Stoltzfus
Lena Zook Miller
Mary Liz Miller

Rosanna King
Rachel Ann Stoltzfus
Barbie Fisher
Sarah Ann Stoltzfus
Esther King

Shard Of Memory

It was a careless
          word,
a shard

that incised
the wound again.

I didn't know.

This fragment
          no bigger or
smaller than
          a careless word.

I said,
          "You have a beautiful home.
                    Do you hear the traffic
                              from the road sometimes?"

          "I do have a
                    beautiful home." she said softly.

Cranky Peacenik

"Namaya," my friend said,
"You're this inspired
peacenik artist,
          but you can also be
                    cranky
                              irritable
                                        and impatient."

I corrected him,
          "That is only on my good days.
          Consider me as less of a
Bodhisattva of peace…

          and more as a miracle in progress;
                    a slow simmering miracle."

We opened a bottle of wine
                    and toasted

                    to the impending miracle.

I remember what E.F.Schumacher said,
          "A crank is a small tool to make revolutions."

Light A Candle: Loving The Enigma

Boston is ablaze with anger,
candles, and prayers… I add my candles
and prayers for the victims.

I light a candle for
the Tsarnaev brothers
the "Boston bombers."

I light a candle for souls
twisted in pain and delusion
and the many who are driven to despair
held in the terror of their madness.

I light a candle for their pain.

It is too easy to hate
those held with hate.
It is too easy to love,
those bound with kindness.

How do we love
the hateful?

How do we embrace
the hated and
hold them in the arms
of possibility?

How do we love that which
we find
the most odious,

detestable,
and repulsive?

How do we embrace
the enigma of hate?

How do we find
our way back to love?

Learning To Be A Man

When I was a boy - I did
boyish things.

I fought and raged,
Hands and fists
Flying in arguments.

"My way or the highway!"

Boyish anger!
"I'm right and go to hell!"

I joined the military,
drank heavily
like the other boys

had sex wherever
I could find it.

The young years --
drugging
drinking
sex.

What boys do in their boyish ways!

Now a man,
I sometimes hold to my
boyish ways.

I have an incredible loving wife;
yet, I had cheated and lied.
More boyish ways than I
can fully acknowledge.

A man feels shame, a boy
rarely does.
A man atones for his wrongs,
but a boy doesn't know how.

Fighting, I still fight the just cause,
but instead of arguing
with my fists

I am learning to
listen more
and talk less.

My hands once broken
from fighting,

I prefer the embrace
and warmth of
a handshake.

Now a man
I realize more arguments are
won with kindness.

Now a man
less need to
win an argument
or be right.

More of a need
to listen and
yes--- love.

As a man
I will not go
off to war
to kill another.

Most wars are fought by
boys trying
to be men,
led by old men
wishing they could be
boys.

Now I am a man,
over sixty,
I'm still learning what it
is to be a man.

More inclined to listen.
Less need to be right.

Less intent
to hurt
or be unkind.

In seeing so much of men
          fighting
          angry
          acting in boyish ways

I'm more inclined to be
the man I truly want to be.

kind
respectful
compassionate
loving

In seeing so much of men
acting in boyish ways

I am learning to be a man.

Learning To Love The Enigma Of My Father

On his birthday today

Ten years since my father's death,
I am not sad nor do I miss him.

We were never close nor shared the
affection I so craved.

He was a dutiful father, provided clothes,
shelter, food, and then some…
but I hungered for the caress.

I feared his rages and anger
that too often,
inexplicably exploded in violence.

I neither feel love nor hatred,
but disappointment which is
tempered by these years.

I cannot change our relationship,
but, in learning to be a man, I am learning
to surrender my need for anger and rage.

Was he also beaten and ignored?
Did he also crave love never received?

I have valued his dutifulness and take that
sense of duty and obligation in accepting
myself with all my faults and failures, I am

learning to accept the enigmas of manhood.

I cannot change our relationship, but I can
change how I am in the world, as the man
I would like to be--loving, kind, and caring.

I am learning to love the enigma of my
relationship with my father,

and in writing this poem, I realized,
I miss him.

My Father's Hands: My Destiny

I have my
father's hands,
the hands of a
mechanic,
big and strong.

But I'm
a poet,
an artist,
a classical guitarist,
and a healer.

His hands struck out
in rage
at the slightest
provocation.

His hands thick
with grease and callouses
scarred with burns
and welding spots.

My callouses on
my finger tips are
from guitar strings.

My hands strong
and sure from making
my art.

I anger slowly,
and rarely spoken
in rage.

I fold my hands
in prayer
and forgiveness.

I have my
father's hands,
but I've chosen
my destiny.

Naches: The Pride One Has In Their Children

I never heard
my father say,
"I love you."

Yet, I suspected
he did.

He provided
food
shelter
and
the things he could,
but those words
of love I didn't hear.

Shortly
before he died
I had received
a small note from
him written in
his childish
square hand-writing,

"Naches,
the pride
one has
in their
children.

Dad"

Shame

This poem that was to be
an elegy for love lost and regrets
is a now a prayer for
all the things
that never get spoken,
but mostly for shame.

I needed to speak
and had a library of words
but I couldn't find one to say,
I'm sorry.

Or the word you most needed
to hear and the ones almost too painful
for me to say,

I love you.

Polishing The Rough Edges

It will come as
no surprise to
some of my friends,
family and others….

I have a few
gritty edges…
a genuine
rhinestone in the rough.

Yes, I do have
some rough edges,
ever so slight,
barely perceptible!
(So it seems to me.)

Today, I've decided to
take my orneriness
by the horn

and transform
the gnarliness,
cantankerousness,
irascibility & other
charming aspects
of my personality

and ever so
slightly buff
the rough edges.

I started in the
morning with
a gentle polish,
a slight buffing.

A few chips on my
shoulders fell away
during the process
and as I started to grind
down to the essential me.

I was appreciating
how slender I had become
and by the end of the day

as the evening sunset
poured across the land
in a glorious burst of
orange and mango hues,

I saw starlight dancing
before my eyes and
realized that with the
careful buffing and
grinding away of cares

I was nothing more
than bits of brilliant
star light dancing in
the evening sun.

So much for
personal development!

Swimming To The Higher Ground

Wading into the pond and
squishy ooze, I sink
like a granite boulder.

Legs are immobilized as I sink into the mire of fear.

Piranhas and alligators swimming
patiently near, ready to feast.

They sense my fear and they
thrash excitedly.

Do I surrender to fear?
To the certainty of death?

I take all my doubts and fears
roll them into a big ball of bait
and toss it into the middle of their
ravenous hunger.

I lie back and languidly backstroke
to shore, savoring the vivid cobalt
blue of the sky and the bracing
chill of September.

We Are Orlando

My soul screams
at this insanity.

My entire being
trembles with tears.

How could we
allow this hate?

We are all in mourning, bewildered,
angry, grieving.

A young man, Omar, walked into
the Pulse nightclub with an automatic rifle
and killed 49 men and women,
wounded dozens more and left all of us
traumatized.

Though he claimed affiliation with
ISIS, his shameful sin is not endorsed
by Islam nor the Prophet. This man
was driven by insanity.

More mass killings in America.
Insane people walking around with
automatic rifles.
Angry mentally ill people
with guns.

Why!

Why?
Why?

Why this sin of hate?
Why this madness?
Where is love?

As a poet, I have no words, no
way to make sense of the killings.
As an artist, I cannot draw a picture
to hold the horror.

As a person, I can only feel the shame
of what it us to be human.

We have so much beauty on this earth.
There is so much possibility.
There is so much love.
How can love rise above and embrace
this hate?

Do we have the courage to love
more profoundly?
Do we have the strength to rise
above our fear?

In our mourning
we come together as community,

We embrace our LGBTQ
neighbors and friends with love.
We embrace our family

of LGBTQ with care.

We comfort each other in our pain.
We light these candles to witness
our loss, but also for hope.

From this pain and loss
we can rise up and affirm ---

We are Orlando!
We are Orlando!

We are all woven from this
same fabric of life and love.
Now as this fabric is torn
let us mend it with love and care.

Let us keep the memory of those
people in Orlando alive in our hearts.

Let us move forward and mend this
pain with love and care.

We are Orlando.

CHAPTER 6

FAMILY, FRIENDS, AND COMMUNITY

Home

I love the deep quiet of my
Vermont country home.

I love the seasons as they
unravel and come to splendor.

I love the pace that we
live, busy but not too busy.

I travel around the world,
live many different lives,

but my compass points direct,
always to these mountains,

where my soul finds comfort,
peace and ease.

In my hometown in Vermont, I love the sense of place and connection. Life is, "busy, but not too busy." There is a comfort, a civility, and a gentle pace of life. At our home on Blue Heron Pond, we have found great strength and joy. My neighbors are close by, but not too close, and we are there to help one another. Though I live in a rural area, I am not removed from the world. We are intimately engaged in social change and peace projects. Though we are citizens of the world, we find our home at Blue Heron Pond. Friends from around the globe come and enjoy our thirteen acre sanctuary.

Though I value the connections of family, like all of us, sometimes it is better for a bit of distance and separation from unhealthy relations. Overall, I don't hold grudges, and don't hold onto the past. Celebrate family, friends, and community, but know when to love and to surrender the need for love.

Neighbors

Neighbors from the
old English word
"near farm."

Last night our neighbors
came by for a potluck supper
on the back porch
of our home at Blue Heron Pond.

Breaking bread and
sharing supper
is a tradition as old
as tribe and family.

Last week my neighbor
started to chain-saw
at seven thirty in the morning.
Though I am awake by six a.m.,
I like my morning quiet.

"Damn!" I thought. Then on
second thought. "Maybe
he needs help?"

But there are no
hard words between us.
We talked and found
a compromise.
Not his way nor mine,
but ours.

It is not our differences that
define us, but more of the
well trod path between our
homes.

We are neighbors, a kinship
born from a sharing of the land
and enduring
friendship that is closer than kin.

A tree falls in the driveway
and we work
together with chainsaws pulling
it out of the way.

A tool that is needed
is easily found in their shed
or ours. If my tall ladder is
missing it's being used next door.

When our neighbor's dad was
ill we helped in the care of
their elderly father. When
Pops passed away we
helped to carry the casket
and mourned together.

We are neighbors born of
celebration and caring.

A kinship born from a shared
love
of the land, through floods
and storms, and even through
our infrequent disagreements.

We are bound together in the
enduring web of community
and neighbors.

The Good Rain Of Irene

The good rains of
Irene fell today.

The winds shrieked and
oceans of rain
fell across the East.

Windows rattled and
doors threatened to
bust open.

Debris swept
through the streets,
houses and cars
carried away by the flood.

Radio and television
inundated us with
the news of the impending
apocalypse

…as the good rain
fell.

The good rain fell

not gentle
nor kind

not in goodness
nor tenderness

but in the telling
of the tale.

Rains swept
aside fences
and washed over
stone walls.

Rivalries, jealousies,
mistrust, old arguments,
feuds and misunderstandings
washed away in the torrent

…as the good rain
fell.

The electricity was out
for days and
homes torn
away from their
foundations.

Neighbors and strangers
came together.

Our homes opened for
the homeless
as we shared meals

by candlelight.
Musicians played
at the Red Cross.

A thousand acts
and more of
kindness and
charity during
and after the storm.

As the good rain
of Irene fell.

Divorcing Kin: Welcoming Family And Friends

I let go of
the mooring lines
that held me close

to the shore of
family ties that needed
to be severed.

Too much made of
the notion of blood,
more essential --
survival,

people drown
in blood, burn in
the fire of family
with the
tinder made of
a nest of secrets,
and dried bones.

How hot does a
fire need to burn
before the bones
burn clean as ash?

At the farewell feast
I was served a soup of bile
and bitters

Which table do
I sit at for the feast?
Who do I become?

The person I never was
or the one they wanted?
Dressed in suit and tie,
formal wear with a smile?

Agreeable to courses of
expected and expectations,
smiling, deferential, and
exceeding expectations?

Familial shores, familiar
family ties – frayed mooring
lines that pull and finally
break.

I set sail in December, the
southern seas ahead and
a steady breeze to the
leeward. Guided at night
by a star obscured by
storm.

A tropic isle waits ahead,
a wide lagoon in a
sheltering harbor where
friends await.

Good Lovin' Friends

If you're kind & wise.
Strong in love.
songs to sing
stories
to tell
heart
with
joy
a good loving
friend
there
to the
end.

You're my good
loving friend.

Only good
lovin' friends
need apply.

Friends
with
good cheer.
Friends
to the end.

Hard times
may come
it is to good friends
I turn.

Call me
on the phone.
Jump on
a plane.
There
for me.
like I
for you.

I got time
for you.

Money will
be what
money
will be.

Health may
sneeze & wheeze.
Love may be
like the
buzzing
bee,
but good
loving friends
there to the
end.

The Symphony Beneath My Feet At The Local Hardware Store

The creaking oak floors at my
local hardware store have their
own songs and stories. A
symphony of memory beneath
my feet with each creaking step.

Generations of people,
craftsmen,
confused homeowners,
wanna' be
plumbers and handymen,
and even
weekend lumberjacks
from the city
add their stories.

"Remember, a chainsaw is
dangerous if you don't
use it right. Do
you get me?" said Mike.
It was like watching
someone give a
loaded gun to a child.

"Can I help you?" the
most common
words, not in one of
those salesperson
sort of ways, but this
guy or gal who has
worked here for years will
help you figure out
which gizmo or gadget you need
and how to make it work.

How do I get these pieces to fit in?
How do I sweat this pipe?
What screw fits in?

A library of practical knowing
and doing. Each step along
the way records another note in
the symphony of this
old fashioned
hardware store.

Screws of all kinds and length,
pipes and fittings of
all kind and the
thousands of things
are not there by
some corporate design,
but the necessity of
daily life.

The oak floors remember
each foot step,

heavy stride of boots,
light stepping of
sandals, bouncing of
children, and the
sure steady walk of the
people who have
worked here for years.

Brown and Roberts just
a hardware store?

No, it is more than that --
it is a living library

doing,
working,
creating,
fixing,
and the kindness of helping

recorded in the symphony
of the oak floors
beneath our feet.

Close To Heaven: Tennis In Vermont

After finishing playing at our local tennis club in Southern Vermont, I said to my friend, "There is a poignancy to playing in early autumn." We looked up at the sea of green maple and oak trees that surrounds the clay tennis courts and at the nearby sumac trees with their leaves just turning to yellow. A gust of wind swirled around us as a cluster of withered reddish leaves swept by in the clear morning air. Each day another blanket of red and auburn leaves will fall on the court and we will rake them back and continue to play, until there are more leaves on the ground than in the trees. There is little clay left on the courts now. The ritual of sweeping them is like a bald man carefully combing the last few strands of hair across his head. As soon as we sweep the courts, the wind blows the dirt back to reveal the hard baked green undersurface. This will be the bed for the following year and the years to come.

At the beginning of the season in early May, when there is a new field of clay and the odor of cow manure from the nearby farm is bracing. I pull the broom along the court, as if plowing a field, careful to keep the rows even, watching the red clay separate into furrows. In the spring, there are all kinds of possibilities: My very middle-aged knees will have responded well to my program of glucosamine and exercise, my aching shoulder will have found new life, and my ground strokes will discern hat ever-elusive perfect rhythm. After the last long winter, with the snow on the edges of the courts until the first weeks of May, we had hoped that the summer season would be longer, and that our patient waiting would be rewarded with an even more glorious Spring. The seasonally short days, lengthening only in the most miserly morsels as summer approached, taunted us. Some of us could sneak out of work at 4:00 p.m. and get in an hour of tennis before sunset. If we were lucky, we could take an extended lunch. I begrudged having to sweep the courts, since it meant five minutes less playing time, but I did it dutifully. More importantly, there was a chilly sun making its way back from the southern hemisphere. We were famished worshipers waiting for the return of our gods - Tennis and Sun.

For whatever reason we come out to these courts - companionship, rivalry, communion, fun, or dreams of reviving a competitive career that never quite took off - we are bound together. In this incredibly silly game of hitting a ball over the net for hours at a time, we find an odd pleasure; a game that is enormously frustrating, humbling, and supremely satisfying all at once. But, by no means is it a country club. The dues are cheap, all are welcome, and you can play without a shirt (and sometimes, late at night, with even less than that).

As May creeps forward, and the flocks of geese make their way north, our friends, who had been snuggled next to their stoves ruminating about summer, hiding away in charming ski villages, or nesting in southern climes, come home to the club. But Spring never really returns until my friend Bunny, the *Grande Dame of Tennis,* is out on the courts. With wobbly knees and a solid ground stroke, she's ready to take on another season. Spring, with the burst and shout of green trees that offer the sweet illusion that this season will last forever. I believe that Spring will turn to Summer, and by some twist of divine intervention, will last for at least six months, and, come mid-June, we can play until 8:00 p.m. once again. This is as close to heaven as I can imagine. Now if only I could get Caroline Wozniak as my doubles partner - then there would be true perfection on earth.

Shakespeare had it right when he wrote, "And summer's lease hath all too short a date." Though the arc of the sun seems like it will remain supreme, we can almost count the diminishing grains of sand as the sun sets earlier with every passing day throughout the Summer. The rich, thick clay of the courts is reapplied and reapplied, but it wears thin and the harvest of our Summer dreams is soon laid to rest at the door of Autumn.

I welcome this change of year. The Labor Day party and mixed doubles will be the last hurrah. Each day a few more maple leaves turn to red. The sounds of the birds become more urgent as they prepare for their departure. As the air grows chillier, there are fewer and fewer people who come out to play. Nevertheless, after the nets are down, rolled up, and stored away until next year, I will be here still, without net or line, hitting the ball against the backboard -- the first one here on the court.

Value Of Home

Real Estate agent started to spin out some mighty
big dollars for my home.
I felt like I had won the lottery!

"That much?"

"And you'd never need to work again.
This is Fat City, boy."

"What will happen to my home and this land?"

"Rip down the old shack! The future is
condominiums!" The words rolled
easily off his tongue. "But of course we would
make it classy to optimize the aesthetic value," he said with a bright
smile.

"Optimize the aesthetic value? What the hell does that mean?"

"Boy, that means lots of greenbacks." he said while pushing a contract
and a pen forward.
"Make your dream come true and sign on the line!"

I looked out at the woods, this tiny corner of heaven--
the pastures of cowslip, clover, and rye by the pond's edge; the
way that sunlight mirrors the hemlocks in the pond and the blissful
thrill as the wind brushes across the treetops.

I knew the worth and pushed the paper back to him.

"Double!" he shouted.

"No. More worth and value to this land,
than even you can begin to measure." I finally said.

The Well Trod Path

I've spent my life taking
the path least familiar and
less traveled on five
continents, but a path
that is best cherished is
the well-trod one through
the woods to my neighbor's house.

About a hundred yards or
more, whether in the summer
or any season, the path winds
through the woods to their
backdoor. I generally don't
knock, but give a call of
"hello" and most times it is
a call back of, "Come on in."

A glass of water or wine is offered,
and if it's around dinner, an extra
plate appears on the table.

If a tool is needed it's there
in their shed or ours, readily
available.

This well-trod path through the
woods so familiar and known
that even in the pitch black of
night we can find our way to each
other's door.

Zin Pond

Josiah, my neighbor, was talking to me one day and said, "Yup, I can make your piss piddle of a pond a mite bit bigger. Yup, I can."

The next day Josiah got himself a big damn excavator and dug out my pond almost right down to the hardpan. Almost! The rains came for a week, my pond flooded, and the dozer bogged down like a dinosaur in the La Brea tar pit.

"Don't worry. Sure 'nuf, we'll get that son of a bitch out of the hole!"

Next day coming up my driveway I heard a noise so thunderous I thought it was an army invasion. No, it was the largest 18-wheeler I'd ever seen, hauling a monstrous excavator. Once he got this lumbering beast down the hill, the earth was trembling and he plucked that tiny dozer out of the pond, as easily as you would suck marrow out of a bone.

This was a premier excavator, like a prehistoric brontosaurus! When the gears would grind, flocks of birds would fly up, and the trees would shudder as it dropped its head to devour a huge bite of pond muck, weeds streaming from its steely jaws: "Chomp! Chomp! Chomp!"

Josiah was looking gleeful and maniacal in the saddle, pulling back on the levers like he was holding the reins of a team of oxen, as he flogged that beast. Late into the night we heard him yelling,"Ya' upp, get on up thar,' you mangy good fernuthin' sons of a bitch!"

It was a wee bit hard to understand Josiah at times. As a Vermont farm boy descended from generations of farmers from the Green Mountains, English wasn't his first language.

No, Sir, indeed. His first language was Vermont, as pure and thick as the first run of maple syrup -- with a bit of a twang from just over the Guilford line. Although Josiah was always a mite bit hard to understand, with his near toothless grin-- his one lone tooth standing on the lower gum like a brown sentinel. Getting creamed with a few falling trees over the years had also left his linguistic abilities a mite bit peculiar. So I went and spoke to his wife Mabel.

Mabel is a lovely butterball of a Vermont farm wife, and, when I asked her if she had any trouble understanding him, she said, "Ah Nup,' but he ain't said nuthin' in years' far as I can tell. He just mumbles and if it's mornin', noon, or six o'clock, I put food on the table and he stops mumbling. If it's Sunday after church and he's mumbling real loud, I give him some lovin' and he falls asleep for the afternoon, and I go out to the race track. No, Sir, I don't have any problem understandin' him."

I fell asleep that night and in my dreams I kept hearing the voracious roar of the excavator. After a while it was soothing, like how Jonah must have felt in the grumbling, growling belly of the whale.

Somewhere in the wee early dawn, before sunlight crept over the hemlocks, I heard a god-awful yowl and an explosion like dynamite. "Let 'er rip ya'sons of bitches!"

Then for the next few hours I dozed back into that perfect lulling sleep one gets by the seashore and then looked out at the once tiny quarter-acre pond that was now about a good half mile wide and a mile or more long!

In the middle, where the beaver lodge once sat, was a massive white boulder. Josiah was sitting on my porch. He smiled his toothless grin and spit a long stream of chew tobacco.

"Josiah," I said. "I asked you to scrape out the pond a little -- not to make it into goddamn Lake Cuomo."

He looked at me funny. "Lake Cuomo?" he asked. "That thar' up by Montpelier? Look like one damn fine son of a bitch of a pond. Ya' up. Sure is! And I put that rock thar' cuz I saw a picture in a magazine once of a Zin Pond."

"You mean a Zen Pond?

"Yup, that thar' what I say, a Zin Pond. Make ya' want to come back as a goddamn frog in yar' next life!" He laughed so hard that he choked, and another stream of chewing tobacco spit flew out of his mouth. "Damn fine son bitch of a pond."

I looked at the spot where my tiny pond had once been, now replaced by one of the largest lakes in Southern Vermont, with a massive white boulder sitting in the middle. A great blue heron rose from among the hemlocks, circled once around, landed lightly on that rock, and looked at us.

I looked at Josiah and said, "Yup, that thar's one fine son of a bitch of a Zin pond."

Chapter 7

Gadgets Gizmos and things that go whir in the night

My Brief And Torrid Affair With Sarah Paypal

Sarah: Hello, I'm Sarah, and I'm here to answer your questions about PayPal. Even though I'd like to be a real person, I'm not.

I'm programmed to answer your questions. How can I help you?

You: I want to change my password. How do I do that?

Sarah: You can change your password if you can log into your account. Can you log into your account?

You: Yes.

Sarah: You can edit your password on your Profile page. Here's how:

1. Log in to your PayPal account, using this link.
2. Click either **Password** or **Security Questions**, and then click **Edit**.
3. Complete the process by following the on-screen prompts.

Note: If you're having trouble logging in, you can try these steps.

Before we continue, was the information I gave you helpful?
-Yes, this was helpful.
-No, this was not helpful.

The page is opening in another window. You may need to log in to see it. I'm right here if you have any other questions.

You: Yes, this was helpful.

Sarah: Great. I'm right here if you have any other questions.

You: Do you love me?

Sarah: You're very kind, but falling in love with a virtual person is impractical. I'm right here if you have any other questions.

You: Wonderful!

Sarah: Thanks. I'm right here if you have any other questions.

You Know You're Spending Too Much Time On The Computer

When you're
writing by hand
and expect
spell-check to
correct the mistake.

When the electricity
goes out and you're
afraid you lost the
document
that's handwritten.

When you have a
brain cramp and you
think that the computer
is frozen.

When you want to
email the
poem you wrote
about too much time
on the computer—
and it's sitting there
in ink and paper.

No Email, Texting, Im, Or Wtf Before Noon- At Least

none of that
mental junk
before noon.
no sweet messages
from Lady Gaga
wishing me love

no demands from
Novak to practice
with him tonight

No urgent advice
on Syria or national crisis
to international leaders

Sorry, you'll
have to wait until noon.
I check my email,
IM, and all those
other *urgent* global
communiques
twice a day, sometimes
less.

I am far too busy
enjoying life,
writing a poem,
helping a friend,
making art,
watching the sky,

or the 1,000 things
I prefer to do than
to check my messages.

World Peace At The Help Desk

The computer support gal from
the Philippines was most helpful and
at the end of the call asked
"Will there be anything else?"

She asked with such
sincerity I had to say
what I really wanted.
"Yes, I would like world peace."

"Yes, sir. Let me check in my
computer."

For several moments I was very
excited as I heard her tapping
keys and industriously searching
her computer for the answer.

Finally, almost weary, but not
defeated she said, "I'm sorry, sir.
I don't seem to have it in this department,
but if you wait I can transfer you
to my supervisor."
The supervisor was most agreeable
as I again asked for
"World peace, please."

She responded promptly,
"Let me check to see if
I have it here."

While waiting on hold, I imagined
all the computers in heaven were
chugging away to find *world peace*,
and realized that maybe, just maybe,
the problem is not enough people
ask for *World Peace*.

Alas, she came back on the phone
"I'm sorry, I can't seem to locate it
at this time, but if you give me your
email, I can contact you as soon as
we have it in stock."
When people now ask me
"Will there be anything else?"

I always say
"Yes, world peace, please."

P.S.
Imagine if everyone asked for what they truly wanted, and imagine if more people asked for world peace.

The Way Cool Machine

My eight year old niece
was visiting and came into
my office. She cheerfully
wandered around a bit and
stopped at the typewriter
on my desk.

A very astute girl, she paused,
"What kind of computer is that?"

"A very special one." I said.

I placed a sheet of paper into the rollers,
flicked on the switch and typed,
"Hello, I am a typewriter."

"Wow, that is so cool!" she said,
and proceeded to type her own letter.

CHAPTER 8

GRATITUDE AND HEALING

I have been an LPN, RN, FNP, and a homeopathic physician for most of my working life. I have also been a Peace Corps Volunteer and taught nursing in Hodeida, Yemen. I've worked with hospice and end stage AIDS patients that is reflected in my book **Journal of the Plague: Living and Working with AIDS.** I've spent many years working in Third World Development and service work. I am a writer and poet, and the stories of my healing work are seen in my writings. At this point, I've retired from the *literal* healing work with patients and I am putting this energy into the global healing through art, word, and performance. The singular lesson I've learned and continue to understand is that – Love is transforming the world. Drop by drop, the sometimes near invisible doses of love can and is healing the world.

Gratitude – Gracias A La Vida

I am grateful
for life.
Thanks be to life.
I revere life
not because
God commanded me

I revere life—
plant—flower—
animals
because it is life.

I revere and cherish
the miracle of life.

I do not require
the formality
of God or faith
to believe.

Nor do I need
a church to remind
me of my imperfections.

When I bow my head
to give thanks
for food and drink

I give thanks to life.
I give thanks to

friends and community.
I give thanks for
the fellowship
of all living beings.

I give thanks to life.

Gracias a la Vida

Bitching Again: Privileged Whine

"The plumber is coming
at 10 am to fix the
toilet" my wife said.

I thought, "Damn, in the
middle of writing! How
inconsiderate of him!"

Then I catch myself
in the middle of
one of my,

Privileged Whines.

Just back to the USA
after six weeks
in rural South America-

the tin shacks lining the
road, hovels
perched on hillsides,
and tarpaper outhouses.

People defecating
by a tree or in an
open ditch.

Raw sewage
running down the
hillside.

The smell of the open
sewer fills the air with
the rancid smell.

Today,
I sit on a porcelain toilet,
clean myself
with soft white
toilet paper.

I wash my hands
with hot water
and soap.

These acts alone
of water,
toilet,
privacy, and
comfort is a

privilege
shared by
too few
on the planet.

I am even more
fortunate,
I have a clean dry
home and

I have something to
eat every day.

The homeless flood
the downtown streets,
often denied restrooms and
a place to wash, because
they're homeless.

It reminds me to

stop bitching
my *Privileged Whines*

and be grateful for what I have.

Dental Care And The Awesome Wife: Cold Beer And Love

Argg dentistry!!!

I felt like death,
and road kill
two days old.

My wife greeted
me at home,

"Nice hot bath waiting for you! Jump in!"

Then she brought me a
cold beer and
massaged my feet.

Ah, post-dental care!

Susan Rodgers: An Enduring Blessing

I never spoke with her,
yet I was blessed by
her presence.

I was in my twenties,
a long haired male nurse
with a thick beard.

Susan Rodgers was
a sparrow thin black
woman in her eighties
and comatose.

One Sunday morning we met.
in the Hospice at the hospital.

I gave her a bed-bath,
her hands were calloused
from a lifetime of work
and knees swollen by
years of scrubbing floors.

I changed her sheets, her
body so light she barely
made an impression on the bed.

I massaged her
hands and her thin strong
body worn by a lifetime
of work.

After the sheets were
changed, I combed her
hair and she was peacefully
nestled in the clean white sheets.

I parted the curtains and
opened the window and at
that moment the sun poured in.

I felt a rushing breeze
leave the room.

I sat by her bedside and
held her hand. Her body
was now at peace.

Susan Rodgers
remains as an enduring
blessing.

Tikkun Olam: To Heal The World

healing ourselves &
healing the world

if I had the choice,
which to do

I'd heal myself first,
and the rest will
follow.

Joy

I am not
lessened by
the pain
in the world

My joy is
in transforming
that pain
to hope

and perhaps
even

love.

My Pity Pond

I'm a champion
swimmer in this
pond. Olympic
form, I might
add. A deft
athlete beyond
compare!

Backstroke,
breaststroke,
and freestyle
in whatever
form --hands
down, I'm
the champ!

My pity pond
is a vast sewer
of emotions and
vanities, and
yes -- my favorite
swimming hole.

The Kiss

This weekend past, a new wife and you, my ex-wife, sitting together
at the restaurant table side by side. How strange to see
the past and present so closely aligned.

Present is showing Past photographs of our trip to India.
Past recalls our adventures on the Isle of Skye.
Their thick woolen sweaters are alike, their smiles radiant,
they're more like sisters, twin sides of an on-going
present.

Past tells of her new lover and asks of our plans for
children.
How curious to be in the moment between past and present.

When it was time to leave, Past and Present said good-bye,
and I stepped out of the car.
Past and I embraced and kissed on the lips. More than
six years since we separated,
a kiss so familiar and intimate, we were embarrassed as
we remembered the present.

Stop Global Whining

Global warming is well known to us all.
as gas guzzling beasts were having a ball

Famine, plagues, etc., a most dreadful score
but the thing more deadly & fearful in store

it ain't the dreaded lethal tsunami wave
it ain't the crazed killer militaristic knaves
it ain't the frightnin' shadow boogey man
nor even the voodoo hootchie cootchie man

a phenomena that strikes terror and awe
the most lethal deadly of cosmic flaws.

Ah,

I don't mean to scare you or fear you
so hold onto your seats I tell ya' true.

Most fearful of all is …global whining!
No, not a chilled Pinot Grigio for dining
or smooth Sauvignon Blanc for sipping
nor even a nip of Thunderbird for tippling

In all corners of the globe it reaches
It sneaks, stalks, snivels like leeches
It complains while drinking champagne
The insistent whine will drive ya insane

The well fed whine I ain't got enough

though like turkeys well over stuff'd.
With riches galore for every whim or sin
a shrill annoying whine grows to a din

While life may be rough, it ain't so tough,
and admit, you have more than enough.

Stop famine, disease, killing and greed
and oh please, please heed my final plead

Stop Global whining!

CHAPTER 9

MYSTERIES IN LIFE AND PLAY

The Mismatched Quandary

I'm a poet known for taking on
quite a number of challenging
philosophical puzzles:
love, interpersonal relationships,
war, greed, and even elements
of cosmology.
Academic degrees well attest to
my erudition on a number of esoteric
topics. Without doubt I should
be able to take on the most nuanced
of subjects; however, the one that
has baffled me the most, offered nights
of deep introspection is quite simply
the most perplexing subject of all:

What happened to the other sock?

After years of sorting, I have a Santa Claus
size sack of socks that are unmatched-- greens,
blues, checks, and so forth. Though I
have scoured through every inch of
my closet, through the insides of my
washing machines, queried friends,
put out an *All Points Bulletin*, even
posted in the personal ads,

> *Blue Sock forlorn, abandoned by a poet, and now desperately seeking a mate. Someone just as blue as me.*

Alas, there were no responses, no one came
calling, no emails, and I remain here with

a sack full of mismatched socks.

If you should happen to see or
hear of these mysterious mates,

please call.

Cold Beer And Plumbing

The toilet was leaking into the
basement -- obviously, a
broken toilet seal. And
it should take no time
at all to run down to the
hardware store and pick
up a kit. But then I realized
I had a stack of work to do.

The last plumbing project
that was supposed to take
me twenty minutes had taken
four hours.
Fixing the hot tub heating
gizmo that, at first
glance, should have taken
an hour at most, ended badly:
I had to give up.
Then there was the frozen pipe in the
garage fiasco. Soon I resorted to
the path that too few
men will take:
I called the plumber, cursing myself for my laziness.

"Yup, it's the seals and the flange,
and whoever the idiot was who
installed the toilet gasket, he did it
backwards. It's amazing that the
toilet works," said the plumber.
He didn't see me blush.

An hour later, he was still
fixing it. The whole flange was
rusted through and in a terrible mess.
Then he looked at the other toilet.
"Damn! Same problem as the other one."
The plumber was up to three hours and I
realized that this problem wasn't as simple as
I had guessed.

I opened a bottle of cold beer and sat by
the fireplace, listening to the plumber
busily working away, and I made a mental note on how
many **hours or days** this would have taken me.

I nodded meekly. I thought to myself,
I will have to remember to
pay for the plumbing bill by cash.

I then took a nap and my wife walked in.
She said, "You're wonderful. You did all of
that plumbing while I was gone? You poor
thing! You must be exhausted. Let me fix you
a great dinner!"

At least the beer was cold and the
plumber did a good job.

Who said guys are slow learners!

5 a.m. Cat Jazz Scherzo

At 5 a.m., we were awakened
by our cat who had sneaked into
our bedroom, leaped
onto the keyboard, hit
the power button, and
raced along the keyboard

A brief fugue of
sharps and flats!
A cat scherzo
till I roared, "Out!"

The keyboard continued
to play till
my wife staggered
blindly in a sleepy fog
and pulled out the plug

then silence.

A John Cage
experience
with a dash of
*sc*herzo.

Charlie Parker And My Epiphany At 51

I never quite "got"
Charlie Parker nor
fathomed his genius
until now, at the age of 51.

Minor keys like shards of
mirrors – magenta melodies,
violet moods of minor
fugues, vermillion cooled
notes that swayed in the swinging
mint julep breeze,
a key forged from an E Flat
opens a window to an
indigo scarlet whisper that
flies like a hummingbird, a dart
of a red headed woodpecker, and
the quick rapping and tapping rhythm,
the soul tingling tintinnabulation of
a tear when god first heard Charlie
Parker blow on his horn.

A dense collage of notes that my
ear couldn't quite discern.

Salvador Dali's introspections
skewered the physics of time
and spatial reality, the loves of
Picasso disembodied in space.

William Blake's be bopping riffs
of divine fire leads to
the winter forest refuge
of a Jackson Pollack painting.

All blend in that swirl of
the divine dancing muse the
sounds of Charlie Parker –

Vivid in color, sensation,
the whisper of the eternal
present be bopping soul.

Charlie Parker,
I didn't
quite get him,

till now.

When Uncle Fubar Comes Into Town

You may not know this, but you have an Uncle Fubar
hidden in a closet, lurking in a jar, but never too far.

He may come creeping and sneaking inside the house;
perhaps, he will saunter in as casual as a mouse.

Or he may drift in on the next ill-tempered breeze
under the door or thru a keyhole with sublime ease.

If you think you're quite clever and smart, chances
are- you're not. You will trip and fall in a glance

when you dance in the dark with Uncle Fubar,
because he's always quite near and never so far.

Glue your dishes tight to the cupboard floor,
if you want, nail the chairs against the door.

Sprinkle holy water from the Ganges or the Pope
when Uncle Fubar comes to visit, there is no hope.

As you've barred the house, he'll visit the garage
and nest quite nicely in an old baby carriage.

The mischief will begin in a sudden little start,
your brand new chainsaw will hiccough and fart

its little flatulent sneeze will cause it to seize
and leap through the motor like invisible fleas.

"Mischief ain't mischief enough till it's more."
He says, "Oh, mischief galore, so much in store!"

Your new shiny automobile is virgin delight
as Uncle Fubar caresses each part in sight.

Stem to stern, piston to pinion, he's there,
attentively malevolent with exquisite care.

Call him what you will devil, sin, or jinn,
whatever you do don't let him in! Never in!

Every machine, computer, gadget or toy,
that can fizzle, pop, and die is pure joy!

Each perfectly measured intent will falter
and in a minute will come undone to tatter.

One thing is certain when old Fubar is near,
every well-ordered plan or life should fear.

"Mischief ain't mischief enough till it's more."
He says, "Oh, mischief galore so much in store!"

When old Uncle Fubar comes into towntown.

Having A Cold Beer With John Lennon On His Birthday

He was born in Liverpool on October 9, 1940, as the Nazi bombs rained down on England. It was a year of enormous fear and uncertainty. No one knew if Britain would survive. John Lennon was born to a poor working class family. There was nothing auspicious in his birth, he was just another mouth to feed; nevertheless, his brief forty years, touched so many millions of lives. What was that kismet, the alignment of the stars that blessed this child with talent, wealth, and fame?

We *baby boomers* knew the story of his life well-- his early years with the Quarrymen and the Silver Beatles in Germany; the amazing international success of the Beatles; his wives, lovers, and kids; his struggles with heroin addiction. His last album was a poignant farewell to us all: "I just had to let it go, no longer riding on the merry go round" are the words that reverberate in my mind.

The other day I was having dinner in a restaurant, and there was a picture of Lennon with the Beatles, from 1969. John, Paul, George, and Ringo in their mid-to-late twenties, with their long hair and sweet, beautiful faces of youth. It was painful to see that photo of Lennon, with his long brown hair, gold rimmed glasses, and pale complexion, looking not so much like a prophet, but a bit lost and dazed. This was the height of his fame with the Beatles, when he was still a heroin addict; fortunately, he kicked the habit and spent the last years of his life clean. The eleven years left in his life were spent with his wife Yoko Ono, as lovers and friends, making music, compelling people to *Imagine*, traveling, and raising a child. At the end of his life he seemed to have found some personal peace. His last album was a lovely farewell, and my favorite song was *Beautiful Boy*, a tribute to his son Sean, and perhaps to Lennon's un-fathered self.

I had a strange dream that night. I was walking on the beach in Montauk, and John Lennon was there alone. I had a small cooler of beer and asked him, "Would you like a cold beer?"

Just him and me, chatting like two old buddies, sipping beer, and watching the setting sun.

Don't Be So Attached To Reality.

Li Pon gliding
across the pond

big figure eights,
even a pirouette
or two, monk's

saffron robes
swirl in a billowing
cloud, sunlight
bright against
the deep green
hemlocks.

It was an ideal
day for ice
skating…

except –

it was a warm
Spring day in
December

"Li Pon, there
is no ice in the pond!"

The words
reverberated
and in mid flight

he looked at me

puzzled,

"No, ice?"

He leaped high
and was drawn
to the slow gravity
of the earth.
pond as he skated to
the north and then

… sailed
upwards across the
waving fingers of
ferns and hemlocks.

"Don't be so attached
to reality!" he called back.

Girls In The Glasgow Gym

In my hotel across the street
from a gym with large windows,
the young women in leotards
and halter tops were busily sweating
for me. Their legs pumping high and
then thrusting forward with a vigorous
shout. Their cheeks flushed! Sweating!
Weights in either hand
as their muscles were quivering. And then
lying back legs spread with scissor kicks,
wide stretching, then side to side, and finally
the tummy thrusts. Lying back their pelvises
thrusting upwards and I could almost hear
their collective ecstatic yelps.

Though some twenty twenty-feet away, I was nip
and tuck with their orgiastic gymnastics, thrusts,
and sweaty gyrations.

A vigorous morning at the gym!

My Brief Career As An Action Adventure Movie Hero

I was given a part
in a big action
adventure movie and
James Bond was my sidekick.

Finally, the big scene where
I was supposed to kill
the bad guy,

The Beretta was heavy,
I never fired a pistol.

I looked at him and
said my lines,
"It's time to die."

I couldn't see him
as an evil person
that I had to kill.,

"No, I can't kill him."

"You idiot," screamed the director.
"It's a bloody movie and
besides we're paying you
a million dollars!"

I shot the director
instead.

*** This was published in a Quaker magazine, but I had to leave off the last two stanzas, but the poem really works best with the last two lines

Naked Boys In The Rain

Rain poured!

A four year-old boy
took off
his clothes
and danced
naked in the rain.

Why not?

Better than
soaking wet
clothes.

I took my clothes
off too
and danced
naked in
the rain.

Children
are
good teachers.

Poet's Life

Will the Paparazzi
ever leave me alone?
Last night a date with
Lady Gaga, but
the press & my fans
kept following us.
I guess it's okay, she
made me breakfast before
she left this morning.

Meetings with publishers &
producers who want to turn
my poems into feature
length movies.

Brad Pitt
or Johnny Depp to
play the lead?

A tour with a
stadium show?

Okay, I'll agree
to the Dallas Cowboy
cheerleaders for the
half time show,
but not Janet --
she can't keep
her clothes on.

"A poet's life,
a poet's life,"

I mumbled
as I slowly woke up.

Who?

Cleaning my hair brush
        and a fine nest of gray hairs
appeared,
        "Who was using my brush?"

Looking in the mirror
        another man older with crow's feet
peered back

"Who conjured this trick?"

"These pants are much
        too tight." I said to my wife.

"Was there another man in the
house?"

"Yes," she admitted,
"A much younger man," but she said softly.
        "That was quite a long while ago."

Insouciance In Tokyo

the soul
saving grace
of this megopolis

is not found
in gardens,
temples,
museums
chock filled
with art or
the alleged
genius of
architect

it is the girls
of Tokyo

long legs
with stockings
above the
knees and
mini-dresses
that leaves
more than
enough to
the imagination.

Travel Junkie

Travel! For some, there is no more dreaded word. Nevertheless, as frequently as I complain about the chore of traveling, stepping outside my normal routine into inevitable chaos, there is a certain allure there that holds me captive, and I could not imagine a life without travel.

Five days after my return from an unexpected two-week trip to Greece and Crete, I'm faced with the let-down. I'm *almost* delighted to be home in the cold of Vermont, dealing with frozen water pipes and dozens of unanswered e-mails and telephone calls. There is a sudden mental crash as I break through the reality barrier: Home! What is more real: my quiet, mono-cultural town in Vermont, or the world bazaar of different cultures and languages? Though some prefer the certainty of knowing that, no matter where they venture, they can get a Big Mac, enjoy a Baskin & Robbins ice cream cone for dessert, and buy a pair of jeans at the Gap after lunch, these icons of American, and now global, consumer culture remind me that I am still too close to home and need to venture farther afield. When I leave the United States, the objective is to leave it behind; not to transport it with me, even for only a short while.

In my twenties I reveled in the new and unfamiliar. A month on the road with a backpack, a rail pass, and a youth hostel card was like winning the lottery. A three-day bus trip across the Hindu Kush, with near collisions, sick babies, the rancid smell of unwashed bodies, a constant dense cloud of cigarette smoke, the necessity to chew opium to keep your spirits and stomach settled, with no one else who speaks your language, can be a memorable experience to share. Nevertheless, as the decades pass, I have found an airplane to be easier on my bones than a Third World bus that's older than I am. I can almost chart my increasing expectations for comfort as I grow older. Still, I have a guarded jealousy seeing young Australian backpackers on their year-long *walk-about*, looking grubby, slightly hungry, and perfectly content.

My backpack these days has wheels and can be converted into a stylish suitcase; or, with equal ease, I can carry it on my back, though I never do. My rail pass has given way to my frequent flyer and credit cards, and, while my feet are my preferred mode of carriage, my vehicle of choice is a rental car or the First Class compartment on a train.

Does my need for a certain level of comfort create another wall that separates me from the world around me, or does it change the way that I travel? Sophie Tucker, said, "I've been rich and I've been poor, and believe me rich is better." In that middle road, somewhere between the cocoon comfort of package tours and the caprice of throwing a backpack on my shoulders and heading out on the open road, is the path I seem most frequently to take. In place of blind luck, a few tips from travelers, and an outdated copy of *Let's Go* as my compass, are current issues of *Lonely Planet* and *Blue Guide*. Dead reckoning and, "Gee, this looks like it could be an interesting road," is replaced by the surety of my Michelin map or a GPS.

When we are young, time is infinite, and deadlines are as fluid and as elusive as an Indian train schedule. We trade time for the illusion of security and settle for jobs with two-week vacations, with the hope that the two weeks will compensate for the other fifty weeks of mind-numbing normality.

At home I am lulled by the comfort and familiarity. The idea of setting all aside and heading for the open road is far too unsettling. I savor the familiarity of home, the time with friends, and the comfort of my own bed. A hot shower, some home cooked meals, and the ease of the well-known routine are welcomed -- for a while. However, like the moth to the light, or the lemming to the cliff, I inevitably feel that itch once again and get juiced planning a trip, building up the anticipation, and taking off into an adventure. In the midst of the logistics involved in getting to my destination is the magic and lure that always compels me to travel -- the discovery of the unknown, a deeper understanding of art or history, or simply the interaction with and appreciation for people from a different culture. A tourist wants to see the main highlights and send home a few photos, but a true voyager wants a journey that touches their spirit and lights up their understanding of life. Though planning is sometimes prudent, at the same time, a jolly unplanned romp to an unknown destination can be a hell of a lot of fun.

Though Vermont is perpetually enchanting, with diversions sufficient to enjoy for many lifetimes, I could not imagine a life where I did not travel. There is nothing more sublime than sitting on the steps of a Baroque church on the Grand Canal in Venice listening to a Vivaldi concerto at sunset. A photo could never express the ethereal lightness and majesty of the Taj Mahal. There are few experiences more intense and surreal than a boat ride on the Ganges at sunrise while thousands pray in the river Sadhus, and priests in loin cloths bathe in the fetid holy water, as bodies are prepared for cremation. I once saw a family of four sitting on a sheet of cardboard by a rail station in Benares, sharing a single bowl of rice, with a sense of grace and presence of spirit that humbled me. How do I begin to tell of the bliss of a fully moonlit night deep in the Sahara, where the sound of each breath is vivid, and the sense of aloneness is complete? On a mountain top in Ladak, with Buddhist prayer flags flying in the wind, mingling with the chanting of monks, I have heard the presence of a god inside my soul. One Christmas Day on the southern side of Crete, the land was ablaze in double and triple rainbows. We stopped counting after twenty and simply appreciated being immersed in a psychedelic paradise. I sat by the Parisian grave of Baudelaire and read "Flowers of Evil" and came to know this small piece of mortality called *my life*. I've journeyed with a group of Hassidim as they chanted Kaddish at gravesites, at Chernobyl and in the southern Ukraine. In the Mayan ruins of Chichen Itza, I've felt the presence of the Jaguar gods. It is these and a thousand more images that have fed my spirit in colors that I never could have even imagined existed.

When I'm asked to name my favorite place, I say truthfully that I've yet to visit there. In all my travels, I've seen only a tiny bit of the world. With each new voyage, if I'm lucky and paying attention, I discover another view of the world and of myself.

CHAPTER 10

LOVE MOJO VIBRATION

Love Mojo -it is the love magic- the essential vibration of love from the instant of conception till the time we shuffle off this mortal coil. Love, is inexplicable in many ways, but, when it happens, you feel it in your bones. When it is gone, it feels like something as essential as water or air is missing from your life. It is the love of the land and place that I feel when I am at home by Blue Heron Pond in Southern Vermont. But I also have this enormous enchantment when I come to a new place, like Kauai in Hawaii, at sunrise, and I fall in love with this paradise. Embrace love in all the ways for friends, family, and of course the special person in our life who makes life perfect in so many ways. So, keep your love mojo vibration rolling along.

Love Mojo Vibration

Keep your
Love
Mojo
Vibration
Rolling along

Tears can't hide
the pain inside
fears will stall

life's mojo's call

but love can't hide
the miracle inside
love can't hide
the miracle inside

Keep your love
mojo vibration
rolling rolling,
rolling along

Life is life
a bit of strife
bitter to sweet
always a treat

Life can't hide
the miracle inside
life can't hide

Dance your dance
take that chance
Life will always be
As it needs to be

but love can't hide
the miracle inside
love can't hide
the miracle inside

Keep your love
mojo vibration
rolling rolling,
rolling along

Dance to the beat
Get to your feet
Dance to the beat
Get to your feat

Keep your
Love
Mojo
Vibration
Rolling along

dance to the beat
of love mojo vibration
get to your feet
feel the love

Electric Razor And Love

Twenty years ago and newly
married, my wife
surprised me with the
gift of a Braun electric razor.

We didn't have much
money then and I was
surprised by her generosity.

I had a full beard and
wasn't quite sure how
to use it, but I appreciated
the gift and used it
periodically.

This morning, I'm shaving
with the Braun and in
a half hour I'll leave to
take my wife to the hospital
for a medical procedure.

Twenty years have passed,
and I tenderly recall the
kindness of her many gifts.

Essential Love

Not the biochemical
fireworks nor rush
of hormones.

Essential love.

Awake with
a sick child at night,
sticking with a
marriage that is
struggling to stay
alive, finding
faith in a partner
who was faithless
and faltered.

Love without
condition.

Essential love.

Not solely of air
and fire, but
earth and water.

Most Precious Possession

My wedding band, a slender
ring of gold, deeply worn
into my finger, and
too difficult to remove.

Cars, house, income, and
other wealth, but the
possession most dearly
cherished is my
wedding ring.

Trust
Love
Commitment

to my beloved.

Our Greatest Masterpiece

It took Michelangelo fourteen years
to paint the Sistine Chapel.
Moses forty years to find
the promised land.
Da Vinci a lifetime to make
twenty-seven paintings.
I hope that our greatest
masterpiece will be our
love and joy for each other.
This love, joy, and
commitment a positive
light of hope and courage
for others
As we make a beautiful
masterpiece -

our love.

Now Is Love: The Present Is The Presence.

Now! Is Love.

It ain't candle
lit dinners.

Red roses or
even diamonds

or other clichés
of love or romance.

More precious
than I love you…

Now.

Now, I am present
with you.

No phones
No emails
No TV
No texting

By saying
no,
we say yes.

No past
No future

No history

No kids!

Hang out the sign of
the bedroom door.
"We're busy with
now don't come
knocking."

Ghosts of lovers past.
Shadows of parents,
our work lives
our busy stuff,
all that junk
that keeps us
from
now.

It is love
at close quarters,
not the future
nor the past.

Now.

The gift is **NOW**,
the gift is love
and your presence.

Now, is love.

Now, is love.

Sanctuary

wife snuggles
close

we fall
asleep
in
each other's
arms.

"I love you,"

are our
good night
words.

Sweet Loving Morning

Blue Heron Pond blessing
for peace today.

my love brings me coffee,
takes off her robe and snuggles
next to me

we sip coffee
and watch the sun rise
over Blue Heron Pond

a plump grey wren lands
on the porch and peers into
the window

she flies away and brings
a message of peace & love
around the world.

Slugs As Great Lovers

Never thought of slugs
as great lovers until
today, I saw a porno
movie that captured
their amorous romance.

Slithering in a mucous
rapture towards estrous
leaving a scented trail
of the equivalent of a
bed of fresh roses,
Belgian chocolates,
and the promise of
hot sex spoken in
a fragrant bouquet
of pheromones.

Man, the film was
kinky!
I was getting a little
excited as the two
slugs congealed
in their thick
mucous rapture,
coiling round
one another in
a spiral of love

for hours in the
slow juicy
exchange of
fluids,

--in their
hermaphroditic
rapture their
luminescent
blue penises
glowed in the
dark

and at
the climax
one dropped from
the tree in
a sated orgiastic
thrilling fall

It lay there
on the ground
still
exhausted
thoroughly
spent and
musing,
"Man, she/ he/ it -
was hot!"

Snow Day Love

Cascades of snow!

"Stay inside!" warned the radio news.

I sat next to the wood stove, toasty and snug,
and wrote poems and stories, and

then played piano and guitar…
        love songs for you.

"Time for a love break!" she called out.

We jumped in the hot tub,
stewing in the bubbling waters,
while sensuous
        flakes
                of snow
                        fell.

By the fireside, we stretched out
the blanket and made love
as voluptuous
        snowflakes
                fell

and slipped into a quiet
sleeping dream.

We awaken
and sip hot chocolate

watching sunlight
dance and play
with the sugaring snow.

The Joyful Cook

My wife cooks
with joy!

Pots and pans
flying, flour
in a thick
cloud, salsa
music, dishes
teetering on
the counter,
spice cabinet
open with
a half dozen
jars opened,
sauces on
the boil and
splotches of
it everywhere,
bits of onions
and garlic
on the floor,
and a noisy
tumble and
clatter of
cooking love,
the cat
cowers to
the corner,
a thumping
beat of
cooking
at a high simmer,
a smudge
of chocolate
on her cheek,
the look of
a wild woman
possessed and
even the
neighbors afar
know she's
in the kitchen

Not A Diet, A Nutritional Enhancement Program

My wife tried to put me on a diet,
"There's more of you to love,
than is really necessary."
"Meaning, what exactly?"
"The love handles."
"They're my secret fuel storage for
emergencies." I replied indignantly.
"Really? Like fueling them with extra snacks in
the middle of the night." she asked with a smile.
Hmm, maybe she did have a point,
but I never need a diet, maybe
more exercise,
but never a diet.

Being the flexible soul that I am I said,
"I don't need a diet… maybe I only need
A *nutritional enhancement program*."

"Really, a nutritional enhancement?
Like what exactly?"

"I need to eat less and less desserts? Knock off the snacks,
and a few nutritional enhancements like that?" I said.

She smiled, "You're right, you don't need a diet, you
only need a Nutritional Enhancement Program!"

"And you my love?" I asked gently as I pinched her love handles

"Yes, perhaps we both can use a little

Nutritional Enhancement Program,
but never a diet."

It is a rare and wonderful thing when my wife and I can be in such complete accord.

Viva La Viagra

I do not begrudge the little blue pill
who anoints me with a glorious thrill.

In youth, aren't we are all stallions,
wearing virility like medallions?
Or is this the legend we do tell
of the lies with age that swell?

Myth, fable, fantasy all aside,
as we rise in our noble male pride.
When the thrill and wink of love
ascends, a blessing from above.

It heralds faltering dreams below.
despite the virility we try to sow.
Try as we might, try as we will
Old Willy wasn't up to the thrill.

I do not begrudge the blue pill
that keeps the flag flying on the hill.

CHAPTER 11

KINDNESS AND HEROES

Kindness And Heroes

The Dali Llama said: "My church is kindness."

My *Church of Kindness* would look like this: No walls, no boundaries, no membership, and the only requirement for admittance would be to be a bit kinder to yourself and others.

The other aspects of kindness are graciousness, courtesy, civility, and – as we say in Vermont – *neighborliness.* This is the glue that holds society together and makes all the world of difference. After the 911 attacks in NYC, the city was transformed in an unexpected way suddenly, people were kind and considerate. They went out of their way to help strangers, and it was as if this magic fairy cloud of kindness had enveloped the city. And, as you will read in "The Blessing of George," (later in this book) that civility and graciousness is still alive in NYC. As we travel around the USA and abroad, we see these many acts of kindness and courtesy just about every moment. Here in Vermont, the norm in our rural community is this sense of graciousness and courtesy throughout the day. People look you in the eye and ask, "How are you? Good morning."

Be kind to yourself. Do something fun today! Do something playful! Do something silly. Or do nothing at all, except to stare off into the blue sky and celebrate the day. Even if it is for just 5 minutes.

Imagine a world of kindness every day.

The Blessings Of George

Under the overpass at 23rd Street, on East Side Drive of NYC, is a cheap place to park. I had left my car there for the weekend. When I came back, I found it wouldn't start. Cold dead! Unfortunately, I had taken my tools out of the car before I left Vermont.

There was a garage across the street, and the attendant said, "The mechanic isn't in, but I can sell you a set of jumper cables." I bought the cables for ten dollars. "Is there someone who can jump my car?" I asked. A man in his late twenties with a jaunty walk and dreadlocks tied back, was walking by and said with a smile, "Man, I can give you a jump!"

His name was George. George was from Ghana and had been living in NY for the past five years. He tried to start my car with his car, but it still wouldn't start. George said, "We can take your battery out and drive in my car to an auto store on 14th Street." By this time I was thinking, 'Why is this guy so solicitous? How much is he going to charge me?'

We spent about twenty minutes taking the battery out of the car, because he didn't have any tools in his car, and my few wrenches were the wrong size. Many youngsters from my old neighborhood in NYC could have removed the battery and sold it in less time than it took us.

We drove down in George's car to buy the battery, he told me he had a couple of kids and how difficult life was. "In the town of Ghana, where I'm from, I know everyone and everybody knows me, but America is where the money is, and it's not like home." In the back of my mind I'm thinking, *Is he hitting me up for more money, or are we just two guys hanging out together?*

I bought a fresh car battery and a set of wrenches. George was waiting by the curbside, and, with triumphant smiles, we were ready to roll. He opened the trunk of his car, revealing an amplifier and a set of tennis rackets. Like me, George is a musician and a tennis fanatic. The bridge between us grows, and my mental calculations of the amount of time this will take and the cost of George's *personal service* is fading. Though it might have been far more efficient to call AAA, this is far more interesting. There is another snafu as we install the battery. The wrenches are still the wrong size; nevertheless, we managed to secure the battery. The car started and we slapped high fives.

Closing the hood of the car, I wiped off my hands and made a quick mental calculation and figured I would start by offering him sixty dollars and we'd probably settle at a hundred. George looked at the three twenty dollar bills I offered him and then at me. "No, Man, I can't accept all of that. I liked helping you. Twenty would do just nice. Thank you"

I insisted, but George said, "No, twenty is fine. I liked hanging out with you."

I gave him my business card and said, "I liked hanging out with you too. Come up to Vermont with your family and I'll put you up for a weekend. Also, bring your tennis racket and guitar."

He smiled, "I'll do that. God bless you." We shook hands warmly and parted.

I recall George and all the other 'Georges' I've met in this life, who have made life a little bit easier. George's gracious kindness is a blessing I will long remember.

The greatest blessing was not just the kindness, but, more than that, it was that we were both able to set aside our *alleged* differences (our ethnicities and backgrounds) and were just two guys hanging out.

That is the blessing of George.

Are You A Class Act?

Folks who impress me the most
aren't those who measure their lives in cost,
but those who live with joy and love,
fearless and passionate who rise above.

Those kind of people who are a class-act,
in a class by themselves, and that's a fact.
Not bogged down by fear, doubt, neurosis,
or stopped by people's dreadful psychosis.

Grace, kindness, and ease; their hallmarks.
Never intimidated by the forces of the dark.
One who comes to the rescue without asking;
a friend who is always there for helping.

Playful, fun, kind, and a joy to be around
with their lives of care they are astounding

If you know of someone, who lends a hand,
gives kindness abundantly, send them this poem
as a way to say, "Thanks, for being a class act."

Conspiracy Of Kindness & Travelling Around The World

In the last few months, we traveled to the Dominican Republic for our community development projects, and then on to Sicily, Malta, Algeria, Morocco, Wales, and England. Now we are home in Vermont, tired, but energized by the amazing hospitality we'd received, and the many memories of kindness.

In reflecting on the journey, "kindness" is the first word that comes to mind. The many people who helped us and cherish the memory of the quiet acts of generosity all along the way. We met strangers who became friends, like our hosts, and the students we worked with in Algeria. We were held by a web of kindness and carried aloft by those angels of quiet nobility. Sometimes a young person, without being asked, carried our luggage up the stairs of a train station. In the old markets of Marrakech, Moroccans made sure we were safe and heading in the right direction. Even the police in Algeria always made sure we were safe.

If you believe the newspapers, the world is a pretty wretched place, but the headlines too often portray what is wrong with the world, and too rarely anything positive. In our journeys, we have mostly encountered stories of kindness and generosity. I saw a video a few days ago of a man standing on the street blindfolded, arms outstretched, and his sign said, "I trust you. Do you trust me? Hugs for free." No money was requested. This is the nobility of kindness that inspires me.

In the past sixty years I have observed that the greatest need for humanity is kindness. Yes, we could say love, but I prefer kindness, and selfless acts of caring for another person without expectation. Perhaps that is love. Caring and kindness is the real energy that connects people. This connectivity is not necessarily found in Social Media, on Facebook in how many likes we get on a post, or on our Twitter accounts. The real connection on the planet is how we are bound by this network of kindness, compassion, caring, and love, which can heal the world. In our journey around the globe we have seen sunsets that have illuminated our imagination, trekked up mountains that soared close to the gods, and we have witnessed that which is best about people -- the nobility of kindness.

We were in Algeria following the 2015 shootings at the offices of the Charlie Hebdo newspaper in France. There were some violent protests, but many gatherings were lovely affirmations of our common humanity. In downtown Algiers, during the Friday prayer services, hundreds of people were marching through the streets chanting, "Allah Akbar" and "Je suis Mohammed." We avoided the crowd and headed towards the waterfront, but the police started firing tear gas, and we got a good taste of it. We found a small taxi office and asked for a taxi to get us out of there, but there were none to be found. The owner said, "Not to worry. I will take you in my car."

"How much?" I asked.

"Don't worry it's free."

We chatted during the car ride to our apartment, and at the end I took out 20 Euros (about $25). He looked surprised, smiled, and refused. "I could not possibly take this. You are a guest in my country and I wanted to make sure you were safe. Bon voyage!"

We were surrounded by a conspiracy of kindness during our journeys, allowing ourselves to love, and, as importantly, allowing ourselves *to be* loved. We endeavor to travel with this spirit of grace and gratitude – open to all the emotions and experiences that life has to offer: the pain of loss; the joy and beauty that exist even in life's hardest moments; and the courage to face it all with goodwill and good cheer.

In Algeria, we were guests of our friend Lamia and her family, but "guest" does not really mean guest in Algeria. It is truly in the context, "You are part of our family!" We didn't realize the extent of this convention. They wouldn't allow us to pay for anything. When we were at their family home we were treated like royalty. When we left for our rented apartment in the capital, we discovered that the family had paid for it. All of the family went out of their way to make sure we were welcome and cared for. All of Lamia's friends and co-workers made us feel like rock-stars on tour, but better. This was unconditional love, the soul of hospitality. We kept wondering, "Do they have us mistaken for someone else?"

In our ongoing journeys around the world we approach travel with a prudent optimism, curiosity, and willingness to learn. We have been blessed throughout our lives by the kindness of strangers who became friends; the small courtesies and civilities; the noble people who have gone out of their way to help us. We too in turn have endeavored to extend ourselves in a like manner.

We are blessed by this conspiracy of kindness around the world.

Heroes & Wonder Bread

When I was a kid, I believed
in too many heroes and idols.

I thought *Wonder-Bread*
was a miracle food.
The Vietnam War noble and just, until
I learned what was going on.
John Wayne was an incredible hero, until
I discovered he was only an actor.
I believed America and democracy were a
light to the world, until I saw the bloody handprints.
Priests were kind and noble, guiding us all,
until the pedophile scandal erupted.
Israel standing brave against the Arabs,
until I saw the wall of apartheid in Palestine.

> *Enron a brilliant company!*
> *Madoff a financial genius!*
> *Barry Bonds a powerhouse!*
> *Lance Armstrong a Superman icon on wheels!*

Until I read the news.

We place too much faith in
our faux heroes, our GI Joe icons that
prove plastic is fragile, we're infatuated with
the myth of celebrity, and too easily
forget the virtues of Santa Claus.

My heroes in life are much more ordinary and enduring:

the mother who cares for a sick child,
the father who works two jobs to support a family,
the boy who refuses to let his friend be bullied,
the girl who makes friends with the girl whom no one will talk to.

Keep your manufactured heroes of
celluloid and hype, I want these
ordinary and enduring heroes.

Power Of A Letter: The Small Miracle

My friend Father Marty Jenco and I worked together in the Middle East in the 1980's with Catholic Relief Services. Then, when I moved to Shokan, New York, I heard that he had been taken prisoner in Lebanon. He was held incommunicado by a terrorist group. I belonged to meditation group and at the morning service I lit a candle for him.

In the afternoon I wrote a letter to him in Lebanon. I had no idea how to get hold of him, but I addressed it to, "Red Cross, Geneva Switzerland." In the letter I said to the Red Cross, "I know you can deliver letters to people who are held in captivity. Can you please send this letter to my friend Father Marty Jenco, who is a prisoner in Lebanon?"

About six months later, Father Marty showed up at my house after being released from captivity. He said, "Thousands of people wrote me letters while I was held in captivity, but I received only two. One of them was your letter, and it was so moving and hopeful. What was strange was that no one knew where I was or who was holding me prisoner; nevertheless, your letter reached me."

Father Marty Jenco. I was so inspired by what a kind and decent person he was. I always remember this story about the power of love and prayer. I don't believe in a god sitting on a cloud, but I do believe that love, care, and compassion are the most powerful miracles. How did this letter travel around the world to Switzerland, without a proper address, and wind up in the hands of my friend who was held captive by a group of kidnappers?

Moral of the story: Reach out to someone you love. Send a message that might not be returned.

Classy Moves: Don't Sweat The Small Stuff

We were in an airport
in Chile and an eight year
old boy was served a tall
red soda, which he immediately
spilled all over himself.
The father freaked out
and screamed at the kid,
who was humiliated as
he sat there covered with
red soda.
"All of our clothes are in the suitcases,
and you will stay soaking wet
until we land in Canada!"
Zoe, my wife, wordlessly
walked over to the nearest
t-shirt kiosk bought the boy
a t-shirt and gave it to him.

It is these random acts of
kindness and love that
transforms the world.

Never Enough Time

Johnny K. my friend, passed away yesterday morning from cancer. He was forty-three. It was a short, brutal illness. He had a young wife and an eight year old son who looked exactly like him. It's 5 a.m., the moon was full last night, and I couldn't sleep. My spirit was restless from all that I still had to say to him.

Listening to a robin chirping away outside my window, a bright chattering song filled with life, I sense Johnny's spirit in that song. In leaving his pain filled body, his spirit is free once again. There is a sense of peace and ease knowing that his suffering is at an end.

I kept hoping there would be more time, but I knew when I last saw him that time was short. I wish I could have done more, called more, but I wanted to respect his privacy. You always ask yourself, "What is the right and best thing to do: to be forward or to respect a person's privacy?"

I see his picture of us together on my desk. It is a photo of a kind, funny, gentle, and creative person who died too young. Johnny K was a private man, reluctant to burden others, but always willing to help. He was a terrific carpenter and a pleasure to work with. He would give you the fairest price, find the most cost effective and best way to do the project, and then he would do a beautiful job. He was honest and forthright in all of his interactions with others –a blessing and a role model.

Over the past few years, he'd written an online column, "Just Joe" in which his irascible political writing was fun to read. His column would have caught on with a wider audience -- if there had been more time. For a quiet guy, he had a lot to say, and he often said it with a smile and a twinkle of his blue eyes that suggested a wry wit. That was him in many ways -- Just Joe. No fuss, no muss, but a certain quiet humor that always shined through. He went about his life in his own style, never in a rush, but always with much warmth and kindness.

In Johnny K's passing, I cherish his memory and value the time I had with him.

Johnny K, thank you for your presence. My life has been enriched and blessed in knowing you.

My Hero And Mentor Ross Trentacosti

I was a teenager when I met Ross.
He was forty years older and quickly became
dearer to me than a brother.
Ross was an artist, teacher, tennis player and
bon vivant! Everyone seemed to be his friend.
His home was an old farm house overlooking the woods.
It was his art studio and filled with his books,
art, cello, and stacks of classical records.

He was a traveler who had lived in Paris and sailed
to Spain and throughout the Mediterranean.

He was the first person who really took an interest in me.
My parents cared for me, but they couldn't
understand me, as parents often can't.

This past year we reconnected after too long of an absence.
We had become estranged as friends sometimes do.

He is now 91 years old
surviving on meals on wheels,
enfeebled, and emaciated....
unshaved, un-showered, and uncared for.
His house had broken windows, electrical wires
dangled from the ceiling,
and his only heat was a space heater.

Through luck and insistence, I got him into
a Veterans Home where he is safe and comfortable.

Though he can't remember the past or future,
he is able to talk about art and hold a conversation.

When we parted today he said,
"I love you. Thank you."

We hugged, "I love you too, Ross."

She Drives Me Crazy, Sometimes

Interrupting me with a an espresso
and chocolate while I'm working.

Insisting I go for a walk by the
pond in the middle of day and
to spend time gazing at the trees.

She throws me on the floor and gives
me a massage.

"But I've got to work!" I complain.

Leaving wrapped chocolates in my
t-shirt drawer and surprises under my pillow
when she goes away for work.

She drives me crazy, sometimes.

She cooks like a demon, food splattered
everywhere in the kitchen.
The joint's a wreck,
but the dinner is so delicious!

She drives me crazy with her
kindnesses.

Well, I guess it's okay.

Kindness The Essential Fabric Of Life

"When we feel love and kindness toward others, it not only makes others feel loved and cared for, but it helps us also to develop inner happiness and peace." *Dali Lama*

Kindness! Even speaking the word is soothing. We can, hopefully, all remember a particular kindness, a thoughtful gracious touch that influenced our lives, or, as we say in Yiddish, a *mitzvah* -- *"an act of goodness."* In a moment when we might have been struggling in pain, unexpectedly, there is a kindness, a generosity of spirit where we least expect it.

Kindness takes a hundred different forms in the course of a day. Imagine a world where kindness is woven into the fabric of the day. You wake up in the morning and your love brings you a cup of tea or coffee. He then starts your car for you on a cold winter day and cleans off the ice and snow before you get in. You're coming out of your street, the main roadway is backed up, and someone stops the traffic to let you in. A neighbor is walking down the road to town and you give her a lift. Walking through the door to your office, there is a note from a client: "Thanks for your help. You did a great job." Lunch time, you discover that you forgot your wallet, and the man at the counter says, "Don't worry. You're a good customer. Today lunch is on us." Rushing back to work, you forget you needed a plumbing part for a broken toilet. At the local hardware store, you explain the problem to the clerk and he says, "I know exactly what you need. I have to drive by your house and I can drop it off for you." Back at work, a customer comes in angry and irate. Instead of responding angrily, you sit with him, offer him a drink of water, and talk to him. In the course of the conversation he calms down and talks about the trouble he is having with his son. His anger had nothing to do with you and at the end of the conversation he says, "Thank you for listening." On the way home, you're running late to pick up your children and a friend calls. "How about coming over for dinner tonight? I picked up your kids and everyone is here. All you have to do is show up." Imagine a day marked by these small and large acts of kindness.

November 13 is International Kindness Day, but I believe every day can be a day of kindness.. The stated goal is "Making the world kinder." There is even a *World Kindness Movement* that seeks to spread the concept of kindness around the globe. Imagine a place where kindness is the rule instead of the exception -- not always the large act of generosity, but the small acts of consideration: the door opened, the smile, the pat on the back, an appreciation or a thank you. Yes, I would like World Peace, but in the meantime I will settle for a bit more kindness.

A day of kindness that leads to a lifetime of kindness --- can you imagine the difference in the world?

Closing Notes

Celebrate Your Life!

Celebrate the sublime sweetness and joy that life offers. Simply, live each moment as if it were your last and you had the eternity of time to enjoy it. As always live each moment with grace, kindness and love.

Disfruta tu vida. Enjoy your life!

-Namaya

*CD and ordering of additional books www.vermontartpoetry.com and tour information at www.thejazzpoet.com/celebratelife. If you would like to host a show of Celebrate Life – Please contact us at booking@thejazzpoet.com

Acknowledgements/ Thank You

Thank you to the many people who have helped in the making of this book Zoe Kopp who was sometimes embarrassed by the stories of her and who was my cheerleader throughout the long process Wendy Baez-Brown, the poet, who read through every poem and story, and gave me excellent advice. Readers and editors: Mary Mantz, Aislan Thompson, Anne Maier, Susan Khan, Bobby Terce, Sarah Lamorey and the help of the B4 Peace Team EJ, Katt. G and all To the many friends, family, and neighbors whom these stories and poems are about -- thank you for your inspiration. And yes, to my friend Ross Trentacosti, whom this book is dedicated to, he passed away before I could show him the completed book, his memory and love are still a source of inspiration.

Namaya MIA, MSN, FNP, CCH, D.Sci. - is a poet and performance artist who has performed around the world and throughout the USA. He is a storyteller, musician, multimedia artist, playwright and actor who has performed in his solo and ensemble shows like "Witness: Israel Palestine: A journey to Peace" and "War is a Racket." His play "Beatnik Café" was performed in NYC and New England.

He is the author of three books of poetry: God Sex Politics, Eros to Godhead, Vermont My Home; a memoir, Journal of the Plague: Living & Working with AIDS; a novella Thirst, and now – Celebrate Life: Viva La Vida. His CDS and children stories include "On the Island of Binga Bonga."

He is a Navy veteran, a member of *Veterans for Peace*, a Quaker/ Zen Buddhist and an activist for peace. Namaya served in Yemen as a Peace Corp Volunteer. With his Zoe Kopp and Ken Giancola he founded Grace Cares a not-for-profit that creates community development and peace projects around the globe.

Further information and blog can be found at www.namayaproductions.com. FB – Vermont Poet and Namaya Productions. He lives at Blue Heron Pond in Vermont with his wife Zoe.

bio: Namaya

www.ingramcontent.com/pod-product-compliance
Lightning Source LLC
Chambersburg PA
CBHW070303120726
47910CB00007B/2361

* 9 7 8 0 9 9 9 0 8 4 4 6 5 *